THE COLOUR *of* IRELAND 2

BRINGING IRELAND'S PAST TO LIFE 1880–1980

First published in the UK in 2023
by Black & White Publishing Ltd
Nautical House, 104 Commercial Street, Edinburgh, EH6 6NF

A division of Bonnier Books UK
4th Floor, Victoria House, Bloomsbury Square, London, WC1B 4DA
Owned by Bonnier Books
Sveavägen 56, Stockholm, Sweden

A CIP catalogue record for this book is available from the British Library.

1 3 5 7 9 10 8 6 4 2

ISBN: 978 1 78530 479 8

Layout by Black & White
Printed and bound in China

www.blackandwhitepublishing.com

THE COLOUR *of* IRELAND 2

BRINGING IRELAND'S PAST TO LIFE 1880–1980

ROB CROSS

BLACK & WHITE PUBLISHING

---

*To my dearest Fiona, my mother and father, Noreen and Pat,
my sisters, Sinéad, Mary, and Siobhán, and my brother, Brian.*

*Thank you for your continued support and encouragement
throughout my life.*

CONTENTS

INTRODUCTION

Joe Duffy

As you read this, your camera is no more than a few inches away, and your 'smartphone', which takes colour photos, allows you to instantly see the final results.

Your photo is stored in the 'cloud' forever more – and you can alter, edit, and send it anywhere in the world within nanoseconds.

It's a far cry from the photographs featured in this wonderful project. Even though many of the photos were taken just over a hundred years ago, the difference in the process, equipment, and recording could not be greater. If the past is another country, well, the difference in photography as illustrated here and the world of photography today is the journey from here to Mars and back!

You are about to embark on a wonderful journey through the cultural, social and political history of Ireland.

I love the idea behind the colourisation of these black and white photos: the detail painstakingly uncovered by Rob Cross adds layers to our understanding of the lives of our recent relatives.

We go to art galleries to see wonderful masterpieces in glorious colour, so the idea of colourising black and white photographs is a natural, if difficult, process. Once again Rob Cross has turned a labour of love into a remarkable public record that will be treasured through the ages.

Nearly every photograph in this volume, through colourisation, invites us to revisit the past with extra detail and intensified understanding and curiosity. The wonderful photograph taken in front of Dundalk Courthouse (p. 92) nearly 150 years ago of a Burns Cutler has so much detail from a truly bygone age that, like many photos colourised here, it is worthy of an essay in itself.

Only in the photo of Michael Collins' funeral cortège (p. 70) processing up Dublin's O'Connell Street do you get a sense of how many people – half a million – turned out for this seismic event in our history, just as the photo of the nearby Gresham Hotel, ablaze in the same year, reminds us that there was actually a savage Battle of Dublin a century ago!

It was only when I saw the beautifully colourised photo (p. 124) of the Allihies Copper mine that I realised at one stage over 1,600 people were employed below ground in beautiful West Cork since 1812!

The image of soldiers in Cobh (p. 117) preparing

You are about to embark on a wonderful journey through the cultural, social and political history of Ireland.

the rows of coffins for some of the 1,198 victims of the *Lusitania* reminds us of why this horrific war crime led to the United States entering the First World War, which through the collapsing dominoes of history led to the Treaty of Versailles and the seething German anger which in turn led to the rise of Hitler and the Second World War.

As Patrick Kavanagh would memorably record in his poem 'Epic': 'Gods make their own importance.' The great Monaghan poet of course features here (p. 84), pictured on Bloomsday in 1954 – complete with crumpled brown socks!

As we travel around the country, county by county, in this mesmerising treasure trove, look at the oldest coloured wedding photograph (p. 165) of Ester Levin (22) to Myer Stein (25) outside the County Waterford courthouse in 1901; every face tells a story, the lives of five generations ago comes to life.

In the same section, (p. 140) the colourisation of the iconic Christy Ring moment from the 1962 Munster hurling semi-final between his native Cork and Waterford turns a blurred black and white photograph into a beautifully composed image of balletic warriors in full flight, as if in a magnificent Italian baroque masterpiece worthy of Caravaggio. If it was a painting it would comfortably hang beside the Italian genius in our National Gallery as an iconic image of our unique sporting and political history.

If you need more images of human endeavour against the odds, go to p. 108 to witness 14 men – all bar one wearing dark caps – pose elegantly with the master stonemason James Kavanagh (appropriately in a different-coloured cap), in the mammoth reconstruction of Fastnet Lighthouse 13km off the Cork coast in the eye of the wild Atlantic. This almost superhuman project began in 1897 and was completed seven long years later!

Beware, while many images in this collection will generate reflection and wonderment, others will inspire anger.

On p. 41 you will see for the first time magnificent

coloured images of the majestic Church of Ireland Training College in Kildare Street in Dublin, built in 1886.

Thankfully Rob spares us an image of the site today, a few hundred yards from our national parliament; the space is now occupied by the Headquarters of the Department of Agriculture, Food and Marine.

Renowned as the site of farmer protests where sheep were herded into the reception area before they promptly scattered back to the open air of Kildare Street, no doubt our woolly friends were horrified by the hideousness of the building – described in one Irish Architectural website recently as being 'attractive because of its ugliness'!

Reminders of national tragedies feature too. In Donegal in 1900, a violent storm dislodged the magnificent Owencarrow viaduct, resulting in a rail disaster which claimed four lives (p. 231).

On the next page you will see a beautifully restored photo of the tranquil village of Creeslough in 1900 – today that village, a few miles from Owencarrow, is seared in our collective memory because of the 2022 explosion in the local garage, which claimed ten lives.

Staying in Donegal, go to p. 235 to see a photo you have never seen before, taken from British Pathé footage. Sitting on the bridge over the river Termon in Pettigo, which marks the border, we see members of the Irish National Army and the Royal Ulster Constabulary smiling at each other, divided only by a hand-painted sign marking the border; its humour and tranquillity belies what that contested artificial divide was to do to our beautiful island over the past century.

And of course there is much beauty in this book, from the stacking of turf in Ballymena in 1890 (p. 241), to the long-forgotten tramway passing Dunluce Castle in County Antrim. Indeed the section on Ulster begins with some of the most scenic and enchanting images in the book before we are suddenly jolted (p. 259) into our recent past with images of the great John Hume being harassed by a British soldier – Hume in this stark photo epitomises his innate pacifism.

No matter where you hail from, regardless of your own interests, I guarantee this book will rest with you for many a long day.

I know you will appreciate the countless hours of work put into this beautiful volume by all concerned – from the original photographers battling against the odds to all those who have produced this unique masterpiece, led of course by Rob Cross.

He has lovingly turned his hobby into a treasured photo album of our country and its people.

Rob has generously and sensitively given us a glimpse into our past, which of course in truth is our present, a gentle reminder that in the tumultuous world in which we now live, humanity, community, and basic common decency will eventually conquer.

Joe Duffy
Author and broadcaster,
Dublin

ATLANTIC OCEAN

ULSTER

Donegal

Derry/
Londonderry

Tyrone

Antrim

Fermanagh

Down

Leitrim

Armagh

Mayo

Sligo

Monaghan

Cavan

Roscommon

Longford

Louth

CONNACHT

Westmeath

Meath

LEINSTER

Galway

Offaly

Kildare

Dublin

IRISH SEA

Clare

Laois

Wicklow

Carlow

Tipperary

Kilkenny

Wexford

Limerick

Kerry

Waterford

MUNSTER

Cork

LEINSTER

or Cúige Laighean *in Irish*

---

*Wexford • Meath • Kilkenny • Wicklow
Offaly • Westmeath • Laois • Kildare • Longford
Dublin • Carlow • Louth*

THE TRANSFORMATION *of the* DUBLIN DOCKLANDS

The Grand Canal Docks were first opened in 1796, following a design by civil engineer William Jessop, best known for his work on canals, harbours and early railways in the late eighteenth and early nineteenth centuries. Prior to this development, the area was associated with lepers since medieval times; a fact reflected in some of the street names, such as Misery Hill and Lazer Lane. At the time of their construction, the docks were the largest in the world. However, they fell into decline within a few decades, primarily due to reduced canal usage with the arrival of the railways. The area was dominated by the Dublin Gas Company's mountains of black coal, as well as chemical factories, tar pits, bottle factories, and iron foundries. Despite this, bakers and millers maintained business along the southern edge of the inner basin. But by the 1960s, the Grand Canal Docks were nearly completely derelict.

The Dublin Docklands area located on the banks of the River Liffey has undergone significant transformation in recent decades. Once a hub of industrial activity, it has been transformed into a modern, vibrant, and cosmopolitan area. This transformation began in the late 1980s when the central government introduced the Urban Renewal Act in 1986 and the Finance Act one year later. The objective was to promote urban redevelopment in areas of disrepair or experiencing an urban decline. The Irish government launched the Dublin Docklands Development Authority (DDDA) in 1997 to redevelop the Docklands and transform it into a modern business and residential area. The initial plan was to create a new financial district that would attract multinational companies to Dublin, such as Google, Facebook, and Twitter.

PHOTO A 1955 aerial photo of the Grand Canal Basin captures several landmarks, including the Ringsend Gasworks, Trinity College, the Gasometer, Customs House, and Croke Park. Notable is the presence of the lawns of Trinity College before the construction of the Berkeley Library, TCD Arts Building, and the James Ussher Library.

The 252ft high Gasometer, on the corner of Cardiff Lane and Sir John Quay, dominated the Dublin skyline from 1934 until its demolition in 1993. The building was capable of holding 3 million cubic feet of gas and was once the tallest structure in the city.

NORTH MAIN STREET
Wexford
1900

Seen here are Harris's Butchers and Leverett & Frye Ltd Grocers and Spirit Merchants at number 20, and Byrne Draper is on the right. The person standing at the door is possibly draper Nicholas Byrne.

HOOK HEAD LIGHTHOUSE
Wexford
c.1903

The existing tower dates from the twelfth century, though tradition states that Dubhán, a missionary, established a form of beacon as early as the fifth century. The lighthouse used to have three red bands, but in c.1933 they were changed to two bands of black to differentiate it from other similar lighthouses.

To the left of the lighthouse is the lightkeeper's house. Six keepers, two principal and four assistant keepers, were attached to the station, with three on duty at any one time. Lightkeeper's families were withdrawn in 1977. The lighthouse was converted to unwatched, and the keepers were permanently withdrawn on 29 March 1996.

ATHBOY RAILWAY STATION
Meath
c.1900

A train departing from Athboy Railway Station. The station opened in 1864, closed to passenger traffic on 27 January 1947, and finally closed on 1 September 1954. The Midland Great Western Railway (MGWR) Class E was a small 0-6-0T steam locomotive class designed in 1891 by Martin Atock, who was the then locomotive superintendent of the MGWR.

NAVAN
Meath
17 July 1904

A photo of the camogie players from Craobh an Chéitinnigh and Cúchulainns teams, who played in the first-ever camogie match to be played in public at a Féis in Navan, County Meath. Camogie (camógaíocht) is an Irish stick (hurley)-and-ball (sliotar) team sport played by women. The game is referenced in Samuel Beckett's *Waiting for Godot* (Act 1).

HIGH STREET
Kilkenny
1905

The bustling High Street in Kilkenny City featuring the open arcade of The Tholsel building. The Tholsel building was built in 1761 by Alderman William Colles as a place where tolls were paid.

The name 'Tholsel' is derived from two Saxon words: 'toll', meaning tax, and 'sael', or hall. On 20 September 1985, the Tholsel was gutted by a fire caused by a small electrical fault. It took 35 firemen and six fire engines to extinguish the flames.

ST. JOHN'S BRIDGE
Kilkenny
1900

St. John's Bridge in Kilkenny City, spanning the River Nore. The bridge was designed by George Smith in 1763 and replaced by a single-span concrete bridge in 1910, about ten years after Robert French took this photo. During a visit by King Edward VII and Queen Alexandra in 1904, St. John's Bridge was decorated with colourful gas lighting in their honour. In the great flood of 1763, sixteen people lost their lives when the previous bridge on the site collapsed as they watched the wreckage flow down the river from the collapse of Green's Bridge. The present-day St. John's Bridge was designed by architect Alexander Burden and completed in 1910. At the time of completion, it was the longest single-span, reinforced bridge in Ireland and England.

BRAY HEAD
Wicklow

c.1885

The collier 'Thomas Ferguson' aground in the Admiralty Dock in Bray Head. The dock was later replaced by the harbour, which was constructed and completed in 1897. In the background stands the once-majestic International Hotel, which was destroyed in a fire in 1974, subsequently demolished, and replaced by Bray Leisure Bowl in 1990. Additionally, the Gasworks, built in 1858, and the Martello Tower, built in 1804–1805, are visible. The latter was once the home of U2's frontman, Bono, and his wife, Ali Hewson.

BRAY
Wicklow

c.1900

Billy Byrne was a significant participant in the United Irishmen's 1798 Rebellion against the British. He hailed from Ballymanus, County Wicklow and was arrested with Mrs Passmore at his lodgings at 6 Francis Street in Dublin City. After being sent to Wicklow Gaol to await court-martial, he was convicted of high treason by the British and subsequently executed at Gallows Hill near Wicklow Town. He was only 24. Two men holding rifles can be seen in the background of the photo.

QUINSBOROUGH ROAD, BRAY
Wicklow
1905

In the background is the steeple of St. Andrew's Presbyterian Church, which was built in 1858. To the right is the Canton Tea Rooms, and the red flag over the restaurant states 'Rest for Tyred Folk'. The advertisement on the gable wall of the house reads: 'P. J. Byrne, House, Land and Insurance Agents, Auctioneers & Valuers. Furniture Van Proprietors, Valuers, Coal Merchants and Undertakers.'

BIRR
Offaly
c.1900

The 3rd Battalion of the Leinster Regiment at a training camp in an area now known as the Fourteen Acres in Crinkill Barracks in Birr. The Leinster Regiment left the Birr Barracks on 2 February 1922, for Colchester, England. The barracks were built by Bernard Mullins at the instigation of Lawrence Parsons, 2nd Earl of Rosse, in 1809.

On 14 July 1922, a small group of Irish Republican Army irregulars took control of the barracks and burnt them to the ground. The remaining ruins were demolished in 1985.

BIRR
Offaly
1901

The four-arch, c.1660 stone bridge that carries Bridge Street over the River Camcor in Birr. The houses on the upstream and downstream sides were all demolished in the 1970s. In the background, you can see A. Scully's public house and H. Flanagan's grocery on Bridge Street.

KILBEGGAN DISTILLERY
Westmeath
1905

Kilbeggan Distillery, the world's oldest continuously licensed whiskey distillery, is located on the River Brosna in Kilbeggan. Although powered by a waterwheel, a steam engine was installed to allow it to operate during times of low water on the river.

Of interest, one of Kilbeggan Distillery's two Copper Pot Stills, made in the early 1800s, is still in use today, making it the oldest working Pot Still producing whiskey in the world.

ATHLONE
Westmeath

c.1905

Market Day on Castle Street in Athlone. This photo shows the twelfth century Athlone Castle (also known as Adamson Castle) on the right, and Father Matthew's Temperance Hall on the left. In the background on the left is Athlone Methodist Church, which was designed by Dublin-born architect Alfred Gresham Jones. The church originally had a tall spire over its west end, but it was removed in the 1950s due to safety concerns. Directly across the street from the church is the Post Office on Victoria Place (now Custume Place), which was the main Post Office for Athlone for forty years until its closure on Friday, 3 September 1937. The building was finally demolished on Sunday, 25 September 1977.

ABBEYLEIX TRAIN STATION
Laois

c.1910

Steam locomotive no.60 arriving at Abbeyleix Train Station. This Great Southern and Western station (now a house) opened in 1865, and the line closed in 1963. The gable wall at Abbeyleix Train Station advertises products and services such as Bovril, Tyler's Boots, Emu brand Australian Wines, Paterson's 'Camp' Coffee, Pears' Soap, Colman's Mustard, and Keating's Powder.

THE SQUARE, ABBEYLEIX
Laois
1910

A photo of The Square on Main Street in Abbeyleix, featuring the Market House and the de Vescis monument. The monument was erected in 1855 to commemorate John Vesey, 2nd Viscount de Vesci, who had been the Lord Lieutenant of the county since 1839.

The original town of Abbeyleix was located near the River Nore, but suffered from regular flooding. When the de Vesci family acquired Abbeyleix in 1750, they decided to level the old town and move its people (52 families) to the planned town we see today.

PUNCHESTOWN
Kildare

27 April 1954

This aerial photo by Alexander Morgan features crowds at The Punchestown Champion Chase. The race was won by Nas Na Riogh and jockey Pat Taaffe, who has won this race on five occasions.

HYBLA/
BALLYNEAGE
Kildare

27 March 1959

A photo featuring 26
men lifting a rail car in
the aftermath of a goods
train derailment in Hybla/
Ballyneage. The train was
carrying inflammable weed-
killer and sugar.

CLONGOREY
Kildare
1885

An 1885 eviction in Clongorey. After eighteen families on the estate were evicted for non-payment of rent, most of the houses were left unroofed. One night, emergency personnel, assisted by the police and petroleum, made a bonfire of the remaining structures in the village.

MAIN STREET
Longford
c.1900

Market day on Main Street. The photo shows boot warehouseman John Boyer's drapers and his boot warehouse on the right side, next to the 1860 Bank of Ireland.

CHURCH STREET
Longford
1900

Photo of the entrance to Longford's Cavalry Barracks on Church Street. The barracks opened in 1776 and closed in 2012. The Round Tower, the last surviving part of the 1627 Longford Castle, was demolished in 1971 and now forms part of a shopping centre.

One of the posters on the wall to the left of the barracks entrance reads 'Recruits Wanted – For His Majesty's Foot Guards – Age 18 to 25 Years'.

VICTORIA CASTLE

Dublin

c.1880

This photo shows the 1840 Victoria Castle (Manderley Castle) in Killiney, before the construction of Killiney Station in 1882. Today, the castle belongs to Irish singer, songwriter, and musician Eithne Pádraigín Ní Bhraonáin, known mononymously as Enya.

The castle was designed by architect Sandham Symes on the estate of his grandfather Robert Warren, located at Killiney Hill. In 1872, Humphrey Lloyd, then Provost of Trinity College, purchased Victoria Castle for £5,000.

MICHAEL'S LANE

Dublin

c.1880s

Behind the clothes broker shops' can be seen Synod's Hall of Christ Church Cathedral and the medieval tower of the old St. Michael's Church. According to the 1901 Census, there were 59 'Head of Households' and 171 residents (including 41 children) on Michael's Lane. This means there were an average of 3.5 families and 10 people per house.

LUCAN ROAD
Dublin
c.1880s

The Dublin and Lucan Steam Tram on the old Lucan Road in Dublin. The tramline, which started at Parkgate Street in the city, was electrified in 1897, and closed in 1925. Because it started at Parkgate Street, it was the only service in Dublin to continue running during the Easter Rising of 1916. In the background is the 1823 St. Andrew's Church of Ireland, believed to have been designed by the Custom House architect James Gandon, who donated the site to the parish.

TRINITY COLLEGE

Dublin

c.1885

The world-famous Long Room Library at Trinity College Dublin is as magical as the library in the Harry Potter films, except without the floating candles or flying books. It was built between 1712 and 1732 by the architect Thomas Burgh and is nearly 65 metres in length, featuring a timber tunnel barrel-vaulted ceiling. The library is filled with over 200,000 of the oldest and rarest volumes, including the Book of Kells. One of the busts in The Long Room (Stall I) is of *Gulliver's Travels* author Jonathan Swift, who attended Dublin University (Trinity College Dublin) in 1682.

NATURAL HISTORY MUSEUM
Dublin
1880s

The interior of Dublin's Natural History Museum on Merrion Square, also known as The Dead Zoo. The photo was taken in the 1880s, prior to the hanging of the large fin whale skeleton from the roof in 1892. The whale had been found in Bantry Bay in 1851.

The museum was built in 1856 to house the growing collections of the Royal Dublin Society. The architect, Frederick Clarendon, designed the building as a 'cabinet-style' museum, with galleries constructed entirely of cast iron.

ST. JAMES GATE BREWERY
Dublin

c.1890s

The old St. James Gate Brewery situated in Grand Canal Harbour (now filled in) in Dublin City. The harbour was used to bring malt in and to carry porter, and later stout, out of the Guinness brewery. Additionally, it supplied the adjoining city basin with water and the Guinness brewery with water needed for brewing. The only remaining building designed by Christopher J. Mulvany, dating back to 1863, can be seen on the left of this photo.

DUBLIN BAY

Dublin

c.1890s

Robert French took this photo from atop Dalkey Quarry, looking northwards to Dublin Bay and Howth Head. Other landmarks visible include St. Patrick's Church on Harbour Road, Dalkey Castle, the Church of the Assumption, and Loreto Abbey.

WALL'S LANE

(now Carman's Hall)
Dublin

c.1890s

This photo shows locals of the Dublin Liberties on Wall's Lane (now Carman's Hall) and St. Nicholas of Myra Church on Francis Street. The church has been a place of worship since the twelfth century. On the upper floors of the building to the right, one can see bird cages, likely purchased at the famous Dublin Bird Market. This market took place in an alley behind The Aviary pub, which was located on the corner of Bride Street and near St. Patrick's Cathedral. Unfortunately, the pub was knocked down in 1963 to facilitate road-widening works at Bride Street.

ROTUNDA HOSPITAL

Dublin

c.1890s

A photo of the 1748 Rotunda Hospital on Richard Casselson Parnell Street in Dublin City. The building's design and its surrounding area were intended to aid fundraising, as the hospital was entirely dependent on charity. Social rooms were created to provide entertainment, and pleasure gardens were established around the hospital to attract attention from the fashionable quarters of Dublin society. On the right-hand side of the photo, a lawn tennis match is taking place.

KINGSTOWN RAILWAY COMPANY'S BATH
Dublin
pre-1894

A photo of the Kingstown Railway Company's Bath in Kingstown (now known as Dún Laoghaire), with the old Salthill Hotel in the background. The hotel was designed by J. S. Mulvany for the Dublin & Kingstown Railway Co. in 1843. Unfortunately, it had been left derelict for some time before being destroyed by a fire in 1970 and was later demolished in 1972.

DAME STREET
Dublin
1898

Horse-drawn trams on a bustling Dame Street in Dublin City. In the background, you can see Trinity College and, on College Green, the statue of William III, also known as King Billy, or William of Orange. Erected in 1701, the statue was badly damaged in an explosion in 1928 and removed in 1929. On the left is the Dobbyn watch, clock, and chronometer-maker shop that traded from 1842 until 1926. In 1855, George Dobbyn was noted as being the Watchmaker and Clockmaker to Her Majesty's offices and the Irish Railways. On the right is the Munster and Leinster Bank (now AIB), which was designed by Thomas Deane in 1872.

DUBLIN ZOO, PHOENIX PARK
Dublin

c.1900

The original entrance to the Zoological Gardens (now Dublin Zoo). The Zoological Society of Ireland opened the zoo in 1831 on four acres of land in Phoenix Park. Early collections included monkeys, lions, leopards, bears, and parrots.

At first, members of the Zoological Society ran the zoo on a voluntary basis and faced many funding challenges. However, in 1840, the society decided to open the zoo on Sundays for a reduced rate of one penny. This initiative was a great success, and cheap entry was later extended to public holidays and evenings.

ZOOLOGICAL GARDENS
Dublin

c.1900

The first camel ever kept at the zoo was presented by a British Army surgeon named William Carte in 1857. The camel was captured from the Russian Army on the battlefield at Alma during the Crimean War. Interestingly, Carte's brother Alexander was the curator of the Royal Dublin Society museum. The museum's collection includes a buffalo skeleton and fossils collected by William, which now reside in the National Museum of Ireland – Natural History.

NATIONAL BOTANIC GARDENS
Dublin
c.1900

The entrance to the National Botanic Gardens (Garraithe Náisiúnta na Lus) in Glasnevin, Dublin. The gardens were founded in 1795 by the Dublin Society (later the Royal Dublin Society) on land in Glasnevin. The original purpose of the gardens was to promote a scientific approach to the study of agriculture. David Moore, the curator, contributed to the gardens' reputation and plant collections. He also identified the potato blight that caused the Irish Famine in the 1840s.

GRAFTON STREET

Dublin

c.1900

The electric-powered trams of the Dublin Tramways Company on a busy Grafton Street in Dublin City, with Trinity College and College Green in the background. At number 108 is J. M. Barnardo & Sons, which has been creating fur garments for almost 200 years and holds the title of oldest family furrier in the world. In the distant background is The Dublin Bread Company (DBC) based on Sackville Street (now O'Connell Street), which was destroyed by British artillery after the 1916 Rising. Also, notice the 45 Stars and 13 Stripes flag of the United States, with the Utah star added (4 July 1896 – 3 July 1908). The current flag has 50 stars representing the 50 U.S. states, and the 13 stripes representing the 13 British colonies.

CHURCH OF IRELAND TRAINING COLLEGE
Dublin
c.1900

A photo showing the 1886 Church of Ireland Training College on Kildare Street in Dublin. The building, which was designed by T. N. Deane & Son, was converted into offices for the Guardian Assurance Co. after the college closed. It was eventually demolished in 1970 to make way for Agriculture House, which was designed by Stephenson Gibney & Associates.

DUBLIN CASTLE

Dublin

c.1900

The Dublin Castle guards with the Royal Irish Rifles, dressed in dark green uniforms, and the Royal Irish Fusiliers in full dress uniform, complete with bearskin hats and Lee–Metford rifles.

The Royal Irish Rifles was created in 1881 by merging two Irish line infantry regiments – the 83rd (County of Dublin) Regiment of Foot and the 86th (Royal County Down) Regiment of Foot. Similarly, the Royal Irish Fusiliers was formed in 1881 by amalgamating the 87th (Royal Irish Fusiliers) Regiment of Foot and the 89th (The Princess Victoria's) Regiment of Foot.

UPPER GRAFTON STREET
Dublin

c.1900

This photograph by John J. Clarke features two fashionable women walking past Sibley & Co., a bookseller and stationer located at 51 Upper Grafton Street. One of the women is wearing a necktie. In the background, the red flag of the Trocadero restaurant can be seen flying.

ROYAL VICTORIA BATHS

Dublin

c.1900

The photograph shows the Royal Victoria Baths with a Martello Tower visible in the distant background. The tower is one of 26 built along the east coast during the Napoleonic War.

To the right is a 1933 aerial photo of the Royal Victoria Baths (also known as the Dún Laoghaire Baths). Originally built in 1843, the Royal Victoria Baths became one of the most popular bathing sites in the country. In the late 1890s, the Kingstown Urban District Council purchased the baths and hired Kaye-Parry & Ross Architects to renovate them between 1905 and 1911 at a cost of £11,000. The baths eventually closed in the mid-1990s. The Dún Laoghaire Baths reopened in December 2022 after significant refurbishment of the baths pavilion, the construction of a new 35m jetty with built-in seating, and the installation of the Roger Casement statue.

CHRIST CHURCH CATHEDRAL
Dublin
c.1900

Dublin's Christ Church Cathedral. Founded in the early eleventh century under the Viking king Sitric Silkenbeard, it was rebuilt in stone in the late twelfth century. The Christ Church crypt is the oldest surviving part of the cathedral, dating from 1188. At 175ft long, it is one of the largest medieval crypts in Britain and Ireland. In the background on the left is St. Augustine Church on Thomas Street, with its 223-foot spire designed by Edward Pugin, while on the right is one of James Gandon's Four Courts buildings on the Liffey Quays.

RIVER LIFFEY
Dublin

c.1900

The crowded River Liffey quays in Dublin City, with the magnificent 1781 Custom House (Teach an Chustaim) designed by architect James Gandon in the background. Also visible is the paddle steamer 'City of Dublin Steam Packet Company'. This shipping line was established in 1823 to serve cross-channel routes between Britain and Ireland. It was finally liquidated in 1924.

NATIONAL LIBRARY OF IRELAND
Dublin
c.1904

The magnificent reading room of the National Library of Ireland, with its vast vaulted ceiling. The library is located next to Leinster House on Kildare Street in Dublin. The National Museum and Library, both designed by T. N. Deane & Son architects in 1884, are situated on the grounds of 1745 Leinster House, the former residence of the Duke of Leinster. Around that time, the National Library of Ireland staff included Librarian TW Lyster MA, 1st Assistant Librarian R Lloyd Praeger BA BE, and 2nd Assistant Librarian WK Magee BA.

UPPER GRAFTON STREET

Dublin

1905

In the background is the Trocadero restaurant, while in the foreground at number 51 is Sibley & Co., a bookseller and stationer, with the 'Boston Dental Association, on the first floor' which still operates as a dental surgery. The driver of the French De Dion Bouton motor car is motor engineer Ernest Duke Watson, while the white car driving away is an early Rolls-Royce.

HOWTH HARBOUR
Dublin
1905

Pictured are Balscadden Bay Ladies Baths, and the 1803 Howth Martello Tower in the background. Balscadden comes from the Irish name Baile na Scadán, meaning 'the town or homeland of the herrings'. The small cove was designated as the ladies' beach, and immediately above the beach was the Dalriada Tea Shop. The renowned painter John Butler Yeats, father of Nobel Literature Prize-winner William Butler Yeats, had his studio in a small, thatched house overlooking Balscadden Bay.

KINGSTOWN
(now Dún Laoghaire)
Dublin

July 1905

Mr Davy Stephens, also known as the 'King of Irish Newspapers', was a renowned colourful Dublin character who had a news-stand outside the old entrance of Kingstown, now Dún Laoghaire, Railway Station in Dublin for nearly fifty years. Davy was immortalised in James Joyce's *Ulysses*: 'The door of Ruttledge's office creaked again. Davy Stephens, minute in a large cape coat, a small felt hat crowning his ringlets, passed out with a roll of papers under his cape, a king's courier.' He died on 11 September 1925 at the age of 84 and is buried in Deansgrange Cemetery.

LEINSTER
Dublin

c.1910–16

A photo of Thomas James Clarke. On 3 May 1916, Clarke was executed by a British firing squad at Kilmainham Gaol along with Pádraig Pearse and Thomas MacDonagh. Clarke was arguably the person most responsible for the 1916 Easter Rising and had spent fifteen years in English prisons prior to his role in the Easter Rising.

LIBERTY HALL

Dublin

1914

The Irish Citizen Army being drilled by Captain Jack White outside the old Liberty Hall which was the Headquarters of James Larkin's Irish Transport Workers' Union. James Connolly, who was commandant of the Dublin Brigade during the 1916 Easter Rising, can be seen. The banner reads 'We serve neither King nor Kaiser but Ireland', reflecting the Irish Citizen Army's opposition to Irishmen fighting in the First World War.

CUSTOM HOUSE QUAY
Dublin
c.1915

Boys catching crabs by the River Liffey in front of the Custom House. In the background, you can see the wrought-iron lattice girders of the 1889 Loopline Bridge (also known as the Liffey Viaduct). The Clarecastle cargo steamship was owned by Arthur Guinness, Son & Co. Ltd. until 1953.

SACKVILLE STREET

Dublin

1916

The wreckage of an electric tramway car on Sackville Street (now O'Connell Street) in Dublin, after the city was shelled by British artillery during the 1916 Rising. The Dublin Electric Tramway Car prominently displays a sign advertising Nestlé's condensed milk, which boasts of being 'The Richest In Cream'.

BERESFORD PLACE

Dublin

1916

A photo showing the clean-up outside old Liberty Hall in Dublin City. This building served as the Headquarters of James Larkin's Irish Transport Workers' Union in the aftermath of the Easter Rising Rebellion when British field artillery and the admiralty gunboat, the *Helga*, shelled Dublin City. The photo features Dublin Corporation (now Dublin City Council) Cart no.8 helping in the clean-up. The holes in the internal walls of Liberty Hall were caused by 18-pounder shells, which were the standard British Empire field gun of the First World War era and formed the backbone of the Royal Field Artillery during the war.

GRATTAN BRIDGE

Dublin

c.1915

Dublin United Tramways Company Tram no.26 passes by Grattan Bridge in Dublin. The bridge was designed by architect Bindon B. Stoney and completed in 1874. Also visible is James Gandon's Four Courts, completed in 1802. The twin towers of the Presbyterian Church on Ormond Quay, which were designed by architect Edward P. Gribbon and built in 1847, can be seen. Unfortunately, the church was destroyed in a fire in the late 1960s.

SINN FÉIN BANK
Dublin
1920

A photo of the damaged Sinn Féin Bank at number 6 Harcourt Street in Dublin City after a raid by the authorities. The Australian newspaper, *The Marlborough Express*, reported the following on 1 December 1920: 'The authorities raided the Sinn Fein bank in Dublin. They tore up the floors and discovered a secret underground safe, which was not revealed on the occasion of the previous search. They blew open the safe, which contained £500 and important documents associated with the name of Michael Collins, chief of staff of the Irish Republic.'

FOUR COURTS
Dublin
1920

The Public Records Office in the Four Courts in Dublin. It housed Irish records dating from medieval times to 1922. However, on 30 June 1922, the building was destroyed by fire when it was shelled by the Free State Army while evicting anti-Treaty rebels who had taken over the building and were using it to store munitions. The building was designed by architects James H. Owen and E. T. Owen in 1866.

DÁIL CHAMBER
Dublin
mid-1920s

This mid-1920s photo by Eason & Sons features the Dáil Chamber in Leinster House on Kildare Street in Dublin. In 1815, the Royal Dublin Society (RDS) purchased Leinster House, the former residence of the Duke of Leinster, which was designed by architect Richard Cassels in 1747. The Dáil Chamber was once the RDS's 700-seater lecture theatre.

Michael Collins, who served as the Minister for Finance in Ireland, leased the building from the RDS for eight months. The Third Dáil convened there on 9 September 1922, and in 1924, the Irish Free State bought the building outright. Unfortunately, Collins himself was assassinated at the age of 31 in an ambush at Béal na mBláth in County Cork by anti-Treaty IRA forces, and never took his seat in Leinster House before the Dáil met.

GLASNEVIN

Dublin

October 1920

The coffin of Royal Irish Constabulary (RIC) District Inspector James Brady, draped in the Union flag and en-route to Glasnevin Cemetery in October 1921. James, originally from Dún Laoghaire, was killed, aged 21, in an IRA ambush in Tobercurry, County Sligo, in September 1920. As the funeral cortège passes, the Dublin Tramways Company (DTC) tram line workers pay their respects.

CROKE PARK
Dublin

11 September 1921

The Leinster Hurling Final in Croke Park. The Dublin team beat Kilkenny 4–4 to 1–5 in front of 17,000 spectators. Michael Collins shakes hands with members of the Dublin hurling team. Also pictured are ex-GAA president Alderman James Nowlan (in the bowler hat) and a smiling TD Harry Boland next to Collins. The Irish War of Independence officially ended in 1921 with the signing of the Anglo-Irish Treaty on 6 December. With the truce with the British in place since 11 July of that same year, Collins was no longer in hiding and could attend public events like this one around the county.

GRESHAM HOTEL
Dublin
7 January 1922

Michael Collins, photographed by W. D. Hogan at
the Gresham Hotel in Dublin on the night that the
Anglo-Irish Treaty was ratified by Dáil Eireann.
The Treaty was ratified by a slim majority of
64 to 57.

During the War of Independence, Collins used
the Gresham Hotel as a place to rest but also held
several secret meetings there. On 9 February 1922, when Collins was Chairman of
the provisional government, he called a meeting to room 85 of the hotel at 7PM to
form a new police force. This meeting was attended by various TDs, 1916 Easter
Rising veterans, military commanders, and Patrick Walsh, District Inspector of
the Royal Irish Constabulary in Letterkenny. Twelve days later, the first men were
recruited into An Garda Síochána.

LEINSTER
Dublin
1921

A portrait of Michael
Collins and Arthur
Griffith. Both died in
August of 1922. Griffith
passed away on the
twelfth, and unfortunately, just ten days later, Collins himself
was killed at Béal na mBláth. Arthur Joseph Griffith was an
Irish writer, newspaper editor, and politician who founded the
political party Sinn Féin. He led the Irish delegation during the
negotiations that resulted in the 1921 Anglo-Irish Treaty. Later,
he served as the president of Dáil Éireann from January 1922
until his death in August.

GRESHAM HOTEL
Dublin
2 July 1922

A photo from the Topical Press Agency taken on 2 July 1922 shows the Gresham Hotel in flames during the Battle of Dublin. This battle, which lasted from 28 June to 5 July, marked the beginning of the Irish Civil War and was characterised by a week of street fighting in Dublin. The photo also features at number 24 the Catholic Truth Society of Ireland (CTSI) and at number 23 Sir James W. Mackey Ltd. (Seeds-Plants Bulbs-Trees). The Gresham Hotel was completely destroyed during the battle but was rebuilt in 1926 and extended, replacing the adjacent CTSI and Mackey's buildings.

ROYAL BANK OF IRELAND
Dublin
1922

Pro-Treaty National Army soldiers engaged in urban warfare inside the Royal Bank of Ireland on numbers 63–64 Upper Sackville Street (now O'Connell Street). The building was remodelled by architect Charles Geoghegan in 1869 from a pair of eighteenth-century houses.

O'CONNELL STREET
Dublin
22 August 1922

The funeral procession of Michael Collins, as seen from the top of Nelson's Pillar on O'Connell Street passes by the General Post Office (G.P.O). People can be seen sitting on the roof of the G.P.O. It is estimated that the procession was three miles long, and that 500,000 people lined the streets; one-fifth of the population of Ireland at the time. The photograph shows that the funeral is being filmed from the top of the canopy of the Hotel Metropole. Originally, the Metropole was four Georgian buildings combined to form a hotel known as the Prince of Wales, but it was remodelled internally and externally by William M. Mitchell in 1891–93.

MANSION HOUSE
Dublin

7 January 1922

Michael Collins and Arthur Griffith seated in the front row gathered outside the Mansion House on Dawson Street in Dublin City with the elected representatives of Dáil Eireann, who approved the Anglo-Irish Treaty by a slim majority of 64 to 57 on 7 January 1922. Also in the photo are Eóin John MacNeill (front row, second from left), who served as Minister for Education from 1922 to 1925 and Ceann Comhairle of Dáil Éireann from 1921 to 1922, and TD for East Kerry Piaras Béaslaí (third row from the front, third from the left), who fought in the 1916 Easter Rising.

MANSION HOUSE
Dublin

16 January 1922

Michael Collins leaves the Mansion House on Dawson Street with his Minister for Justice, Kevin O'Higgins, after being elected chairman of the Provisional Government. Collins was on his way to the handover of Dublin Castle and the formal transfer of power from the British government. It is reported that after returning from Dublin Castle to the Dáil Eireann cabinet, Collins greeted Arthur Griffith with the words, 'The Castle has fallen!'

MARLBOROUGH STREET
Dublin

16 August 1922

The removal of the casket of former Irish President Arthur Griffith from St. Mary's Pro Cathedral on Marlborough Street in Dublin City. Michael Collins can be seen shouldering the remains, marked with an X. Just six days later, Collins himself would be assassinated at the age of 31 in an ambush by anti-Treaty IRA forces at Béal na mBláth in County Cork.

THE HIBERNIAN BIBLE SOCIETY

Dublin

July 1922

Witness the sheer destruction caused by the Irish Civil War on the neighbouring buildings of The Hibernian Bible Society at 10 Upper Sackville Street (now O'Connell Street) during the Battle of Dublin. The battle lasted for a week, from 28 June to 5 July. In the foreground, there is a public convenience toilet where the famous Irish uilleann piper Nicholas Markey worked as a Dublin corporation toilet attendant.

EDINBURGH TEMPERANCE HOTEL
Dublin
5 July 1922

Guests leaving the hotel, located at 56 Upper Sackville Street (now O'Connell Street) in Dublin City. They had been confined there for three days during the Battle of Dublin, a week-long series of street battles that took place from 28 June to 5 July. The British Army registration number 1043CK is visible on the Rolls-Royce armoured car 'The Fighting 2nd'. These cars were given an ARR (Armoured Rolls-Royce) number by the National Army, with Michael Collins's designated Armoured Rolls-Royce being ARR8.

HOWTH
Dublin
March 1923

Battling Siki, the world's light heavyweight champion boxer, with his sparring partner Eugene Stube outside the Claremont Hotel in Howth. Siki was in Dublin to fight 'Bold' Mike McTigue, who hailed from Kilnamona in County Clare. The fight took place on St. Patrick's Day at the old La Scala Theatre on Princes Street in Dublin. Despite Siki's efforts, McTigue (also known as 'Methuselah') won the fight on points. In 1928, Siki was found dead at the age of 28, lying face down and shot twice in the back at close range.

COLLEGE GREEN

Dublin

1932

Maud Gonne MacBride, an Irish nationalist and political activist known as The Irish Joan of Arc, addresses the crowd on College Green in Dublin. She wears her trademark black mantilla as Dubliners celebrate the release of IRA men imprisoned at Arbour Hill Prison during the Irish Civil War. Seated next to Maud is Anglo-Irish suffragist Charlotte Despard, a founding member of the Women's Freedom League, Women's Peace Crusade, and the Irish Women's Franchise League. Despard was imprisoned four times for her suffragette activism, but continued actively campaigning for women's rights, poverty relief, and world peace right into her nineties.

DAME STREET

Dublin

June 1932

The street is decorated with banners and bunting to honour the 31st International Eucharistic Congress. The congress took place in Dublin from 21 to 26 June, and was one of the largest Eucharistic congresses of the twentieth century. Ireland was chosen as the host country because 1932 marked the 1500th anniversary of St. Patrick's arrival. The theme of the congress was 'The Propagation of the Sainted Eucharist by Irish Missionaries'.

THE BLUESHIRT CONGRESS
Dublin
1934

General Eoin O'Duffy is seen taking the Roman salute at a Blueshirt Congress. O'Duffy was the Chief of Staff of the IRA and the head of the Army Comrades Association (ACA), also known as the Blueshirts. He was also the leader of the political party Fine Gael.

The Army Comrades Association (ACA), which was later renamed the National Guard, Young Ireland, and finally the League of Youth, was a paramilitary organisation founded in Dublin on 11 August 1932, during the Irish Free State.

Eoin O'Duffy was informally regarded as the third Garda Commissioner, following Patrick Brennan's unofficial election by mutineers during the Civic Guard Mutiny in May 1922. Michael Staines served as the first Garda Commissioner from February 1922 to September 1922.

CROKE PARK
Dublin
6 September 1953

An aerial photo of Croke Park during the 66th All Ireland Senior Hurling Final, in which Cork beat Galway 3–3 to 0–8. The match had an attendance of 71,195, and due to the clash of colours, both counties lined out in their provincial jerseys, with Cork wearing Munster's blue and Galway wearing the white of Connacht.

Croke Park is the headquarters of the Gaelic Athletic Association (GAA). On 21 November 1920, during the Irish War of Independence, Croke Park was the site of a massacre perpetrated by the Auxiliary Division of the Royal Irish Constabulary, known as 'Bloody Sunday', in which fourteen civilians were killed. The dead included thirteen spectators and Tipperary player Michael Hogan. The Hogan stand, built in 1924, was named in his honour.

CROKE PARK
Dublin
1928

The 1928 Tailteann Games (Aonach Tailteann) held in Croke Park, Dublin City. Ireland's Norman J. McEachern, a member of the 1886 Clonliffe Harriers Athletic Club, is shown winning the 880 yards race. McEachern was also the Irish Champion for this distance in 1924, 1926, 1927, and 1928.

The Tailteann Games was a sporting and cultural festival held in the Irish Free State in 1924, 1928, and 1932. It aimed to revive the ancient Tailteann Games, which were held from legendary times until the Norman invasion of Ireland in the late twelfth century.

DALYMOUNT PARK
Dublin
13 October 1963

Ireland faced Austria in the 1st round 2nd leg of the UEFA European Championship. The match was refereed by Einar Poulsen and took place in Dalymount Park, in front of a crowd of 39,963. Ireland won 3–2 on aggregate, advancing to the next round. In the background, a line of fans perched on an advertising sign reflecting the light resembles a line of birds on a telephone wire.

SANDYCOVE

Dublin

16 June 1954

On 16 June 1954, Elinor Wiltshire captured a Bloomsday photo featuring Irish poets Anthony Cronin and Patrick Kavanagh with John Ryan (centre), the owner of Bailey's pub on Duke Street, at the Martello Tower in Sandycove, Dublin. They had been retracing the steps of Leopold Bloom, the main protagonist in James Joyce's 1922 novel *Ulysses*. Bloomsday is an annual commemoration and celebration of the life of Joyce, observed in Dublin and elsewhere on 16 June, the day in 1904 on which the novel is set and the day of Joyce's first sexual encounter with his wife-to-be, Nora Barnacle.

POWERS DISTILLERY

(now The National College of
Art and Design)
Dublin

5 July 1961

The fire at Powers Distillery on John's Lane in Dublin City. The fire attracted a crowd of onlookers, some of whom were delighted to find whiskey flowing through the streets. There are stories of how cats and dogs were drunk for weeks, staggering about to the great amusement of the children attending the school on John's Lane.

In the background is the St. Augustine Church (John's Lane Church), which has a 223-foot spire designed by Edward Pugin. It dates back to 1862 and was completed in 1895.

MERCHANT'S ARCH
Dublin
1969

A couple, captured by photographer Elinor Wiltshire in 1969, browsing through books in Merchant's Arch, Temple Bar in Dublin City. In the background, at the junction of Crown Alley and Cope Street, is the rear entrance door to the old Commercial Buildings. These were replaced in 1980 by the Central Bank of Ireland, designed by architect Sam Stephenson.

MARTELLO TOWER
Dublin
1964

This 1964 photo by Elinor Vere O'Brien features the Martello Tower at Seapoint in Dublin. The tower is one of a series of 26 towers and batteries built between Bray and Balbriggan in 1804–1805. The towers were built in Ireland due to a fear of invasion by Napoleon Bonaparte, who had already conquered Spain, Italy, Switzerland, and the Netherlands. It was believed that Ireland and England were next on his list.

The Dublin towers were part of a large network of fortifications. Throughout the nineteenth century, around 50 towers were built along the Irish coastline, with a further 140 constructed in the United Kingdom. Of the Irish towers, 29 were built in the Dublin Bay area.

TINNAHINCH CASTLE
Carlow
c.1890

Built by James Butler, the third Lord Mountgarrett, circa 1620, the castle is located on the River Barrow in Tinnahinch, Graiguenamanagh (village of the monks) in County Carlow. In the distant background, you can see Brandondale House, which was built between 1784 and 1815. Also visible is Seán Prionsias Ó Faoláin (1900–91), whose short story *The Trout* was inspired by a visit to Brandondale House.

RIVER BARROW
Carlow
1890s

Leighlinbridge Castle, built in 1181 on the River Barrow in Carlow. In the 1270s, when the Carmelites first came to Ireland, they established their first friary in Leighlinbridge. The town's nine-arched bridge was constructed circa 1320 by Maurice Jakis, a Canon of Kildare Cathedral, and remains one of the oldest functioning bridges in Europe. Leighlinbridge Castle, also known as Black Castle, was built for the Normans in 1181. In the 1540s, a Carmelite friary was converted into a new fort by Edward Bellingham. Behind the castle is Garrison House, a detached five-bay, three-story house built in around 1760 and restored in 1991.

LODGE MILLS

Carlow

c.1900

This photo shows the 1824 Lodge Mills, opened by Owen Murphy on the River Barrow in Bagenalstown, County Carlow. In 1792, the Barrow Navigation Company started a plan to link the town and river to the recently constructed Grand Canal at Athy. The goal was to make the river navigable for boats carrying up to 40 tons by canalising it.

DUNDALK COURTHOUSE
Louth
1875

A photo showing a Burns Cutler outside Dundalk Courthouse. In the background on Crowe Street are located several local businesses, including the Herald Office, Bernard Dooley, P. McCabe, Fancy Emporium, Reilly Hair Dresser, and a billiard room upstairs. Dundalk Courthouse was designed by Edward Parke and John Bowden in the neoclassical style, and was built in ashlar stone. It was completed in 1819.

DROGHEDA
Louth

c.1880

Shop Street in Drogheda, captured by Robert French sometime between 1876 and 1883. In the background is the 1770 Tholsel, which was converted into a Hibernian Bank in 1890. The Whitworth monument, erected in 1876 in recognition of Benjamin Whitworth and his contributions to the town of Drogheda, can also be seen. The monument was re-erected at The Mall/North Quay in 1894 and removed in 1965.

On the left, at number 24, Webster's Bakery, a painter is marbling the shopfront. At number 22, you can see the three globes of Curtis Pawnbrokers, next to E. O'Hanlon's Hair Cutting Rooms.

CARLINGFORD HARBOUR
Louth
c.1900

Carlingford Harbour on the Cooley Peninsula. The photo features several landmarks, including St. Michael's Gothic Revival Church, built circa 1870. Taaffe's Castle, built circa 1520 and named after the Taaffe merchant family, is also visible. By 1661, Theobald Taaffe had become the 1st Earl of Carlingford. The Church of Holy Trinity, which incorporates an earlier medieval tower, was founded in the 1660s and the existing building was constructed in 1821. Additionally, King John's Castle, founded by the Norman Knight Hugh de Lacy in the twelfth-century, can be seen.

DUNDALK

Louth

1900

The spire of the thirteenth-century St. Nicholas's Church, commonly known as 'the Green Church', can be seen in the background. Also featured on the right is Patteson's shop. Originally built as a three-storey townhouse, the premises were adapted for use as a department store in 1834 by B. Patterson & Co.

ANNAVERNA
Louth
1940

Men cutting turf at Annaverna. The photo looks down over Ravensdale and across the border towards Jonesborough in County Armagh.

MUNSTER

or Cúige Mumhan *in Irish*

Cork • Kerry • Tipperary • Clare
Limerick • Waterford

THE
LAWRENCE COVE
PANORAMIC

Panoramic images have a long history predating the invention of photography itself in 1839. Early panoramas were created through painting, such as murals in Pompeii near the coast of the Bay of Naples in Italy.

Nowadays, most digital cameras, especially smartphone cameras, have in-camera stitching technology that can generate panoramas. However, in the past, early panoramas were created by placing two or more daguerreotype plates side-by-side. Daguerreotypes were the first commercially available photographic process and produced highly detailed images on silver-coated copper plates.

Although panoramic cameras were available in the nineteenth-century, they were very expensive. Therefore, photographers manually stitched photographs together to generate panoramas. During my research on William Mervyn Lawrence's photographic studio, I discovered two photographs that indicate the studio actually used this technique. One photo depicts Rerrin village on Bere Island, Castletownbere, County Cork, while the other features the Lawrence Cove School on the top and on the bottom are the British Admiralty Recreation Grounds and the Lawrence Cove Sports Pavilion. Both were taken from the same position but on different dates by Robert French, the chief photographer of William Mervyn Lawrence's photographic studio based opposite the General Post Office in Dublin City. This suggests that the intention was to create a panoramic image of Lawrence Cove, helping to preserve Ireland's village history through the camera for future generations to enjoy.

Of interest, Lawrence Cove was named after a branch of the O'Sullivan clan known as O'Sullivan Labhrás (Lawras or Lawson). This branch was descended from a cadet branch of the O'Sullivan Beara clan.

PHOTOS Rerrin (Raerainn) village on Bere Island, Castletownbere, County Cork. The photograph features the Lawrence Cove School on the top and on the bottom are the British Admiralty Recreation Grounds and the Lawrence Cove Sports Pavilion. In 1898, the British military issued a compulsory purchase order for large island areas to construct additional fortifications to protect the British fleet anchored in Berehaven Harbour.

KENT RAILWAY STATION

Cork

1893

This photo captures the beautiful curves of Kent Railway Station in Cork City, which opened on 2 February 1893. Originally named Glanmire Road Station, it was renamed in 1966, on the 50th anniversary of the Easter Rising, after Thomas Kent; an Irish nationalist court-martialled and executed following a gunfight with the Royal Irish Constabulary on 9 May 1916.

Note the array of platform signage, including the Ladies First-Class Room and Ladies Third-Class Room. Prime Minister of the United Kingdom William Gladstone insisted that a third-class option be created for poorer people, but the train companies disliked this idea as it reduced their revenue. As a result, second-class was removed between 1875 and 1956, and the next best option after first-class was a third-class ticket.

THE REBEL PRIEST
Cork

c.1917–1935

Fr. Dominic O'Connor, also known as The Rebel Priest, was a Capuchin priest who ministered to Terence MacSwiney during his 74-day hunger strike in Brixton Prison and was present at his death on 25 October 1920. In January 1921, he was court-martialled and sentenced to five years in prison. He served approximately one year of his sentence in Parkhurst Prison.

Following the signing of the Treaty in December 1921, there was a general amnesty, and he was released in January 1922. Parkhurst Prison was used to imprison Republicans, including the men sent to bring MacSwiney's body back to Ireland. These men were imprisoned there for fourteen months for being members of an illegal organisation.

YOUGHAL

Cork

c.1900

This photograph shows pigs being herded down Friar Street in Youghal. In the background is the Clock Gate Tower. On the left is the Devonshire Arms Hotel, built by the Duke of Devonshire circa 1780.

The Youghal Clock Gate Tower, built in 1777, was used as the town gaol until 1837, and prisoners were executed by hanging from the window. Of interest, there is a British military armoured car in the background.

FASTNET ROCK
Cork

c.1900

This photo features master stonemason James Kavanagh and his fearless construction crew working on a 54m-high lighthouse situated on the remote Fastnet Rock in the Atlantic Ocean. Kavanagh, wearing the white coat, is said to have placed every one of the 2,047 Cornish granite dovetailed blocks weighing up to 3 tons with his bare hands. Unfortunately, Kavanagh died before the Fastnet Lighthouse entered service on 27 June 1904. The photo shows the tramway used to carry the blocks, which were cut to precise measurements at Penwryn in Cornwall and transported to Rock Island in Crookhaven. From there, a specially built steamship, the SS *Lerne*, brought them out to the rock.

KINSALE

Cork

c.1900

The historic military port and fishing town of Kinsale (Cionn tSáile), which means 'head of the brine', located at the mouth of the River Bandon. Kinsale is famous for the Battle of Kinsale, fought in 1601, between the armies of England and those of Spain, and the Northern Irish Chieftains. The Irish and Spanish forces were defeated, marking a turning point in Irish history and leading to the decline of the old Gaelic way of life in Ireland. The power of the Chieftains and Clans also broke down as a result of the battle. In the background of this photo is the Kinsale Infantry Barracks (now Troopers Close) and the Gothic church of the Carmelite friary, which was built in 1840.

CASTLETOWNBERE

Cork

c.1900

A photo featuring Castletownbere locals opposite the Royal Irish Constabulary (RIC) Barracks on Main Street in West Cork. This barracks was the base of Constable John Moriarty, who was accidentally shot and killed by Constable John Phelan's revolver in 1918 at the age of 31. This incident made Moriarty the first RIC man in West Cork to die during the Irish War of Independence.

CASTLETOWNBERE

Cork

c.1900

A busy market day in the fishing port town of Castletownbere, located on the Beara Peninsula in West Cork. The market was held on the first Thursday of every month in The Square, and was filled with traders, shoppers, ponies, carts, and barrels. On the right is shopkeeper Daniel Moriarty's shop, as well as Harrington's Spirit Store bar (now O'Donoghue's bar).

CASTLETOWNBERE
Cork
1914

The British Royal Navy Artillery fleet anchored in the deep-water harbour of Berehaven in Castletownbere. At the time, the battlecruiser HMS *Tiger* was undergoing gunnery trials. The Royal Navy first occupied the waters of West Cork in 1797, and the area remained a British Navy and Army base until 29 September 1938. Pursuant to the Anglo-Irish Trade Agreement on 25 April 1938, it was ceded to Ireland along with two other deep-water Treaty Ports: Spike Island in County Cork, and Lough Swilly in County Donegal.

COAL QUAY
Cork
1905

Street vendors on harvest day, 1905, wearing their Shaws (also known as Shawlies) on a bustling Coal Quay (kay) that is now Cornmarket Street in Cork City. The Tuscan columns and arcades of the Coal Quay building, a former corn market, were built in 1739 and are reputed to be the work of Italian architect Alessandro Maria Gaetano Galilei. On the left is Fitzgerald Basket Manufacturer next to number 39 Beamish & Crawford bar.

CHARLEVILLE

Cork

1910

A photo of a cartload of milk churns waiting outside the Meadowvale Dairy Company on Baker's Lane in Charleville, County Cork. Meadowvale was originally known as the Charleville Dairy Company and was renamed in 1907. In the background, the Georgian houses on Clancy Terrace include the first Mercy convent in Charleville, as well as the birthplace of Eliza Lynch. Lynch was the Irish mistress and wife of Francisco Solano López, the president of Paraguay.

COBH

Cork

1915

On 7 May 1915, the German submarine *U20* torpedoed the RMS *Lusitania*, a Cunard Ocean Liner, once the world's largest passenger ship. It sank off the coast of Kinsale, with the loss of 1,198 lives. The attack contributed to the United States' entry into the First World War. Many of the victims were children travelling with their Canadian mothers to England to join their relatives while their fathers fought at the front in the First World War.

A huge funeral procession was held for some of the victims in Cobh (pictured to the left). The procession featured hearses draped with British flags and took place on East Beach. After the tragedy, a company of British soldiers dug three mass graves in the Old Town Cemetery. There, 140 unidentified victims were buried.

The right-hand picture shows British soldiers lifting coffins onto carts as the flag in the background flies at half-mast.

GRAND PARADE, CORK CITY
Cork
12 March 1922

Michael Collins addressing a Free State pro-Treaty rally from the podium on Cork City's Grand Parade. In the left image is Michael Collins with his speech notes in hand. On the right is the crowd, numbered around 50,000 people. The first speaker to address the huge hostile crowd was Liam De Róiste, followed by Collins.

During the rally, Collins attacked the anti-Treaty leader, Eamon de Valera, accusing him of deserting Ireland and being absent in America during the War of Independence. The day after the rally, Collins wrote to his fiancée, Kitty Kiernan, saying, 'Everything went off excellently on the whole – no real trouble, all the people for us.'

CORK CITY

Cork

13 March 1922

Michael Collins, photographed by W. D. Hogan, accepting a bouquet of flowers from a child. The day before, Collins had attended a pro-Treaty rally on Cork City's Grand Parade, where he and his fellow Dáil Éireann pro-Treaty members spoke to a crowd of around 50,000 people.

BÉAL NA mBLÁTH

Cork

1922

Michael Collins's sister, Mary Collins Powell, standing at the memorial cross near a collection of handmade crosses at Béal na mBláth. This is the site where her brother Michael was killed on 22 August. The cross is now displayed in the Collins Barracks Museum in Cork.

Mary Collins Powell was the daughter of Michael John Collins and Mary Anne (O'Brien) Collins. She was born on 6 June 1881 in Woodfield, Clonakilty and died on 24 May 1955 at Bon Secours Hospital, Mount Carmel, Magazine Road in Cork City.

YOUGHAL OLD ROAD

Cork

1922

A young barefoot boy wearing a Pioneer Total Abstinence Association badge. He is holding an épée sword aloft that he salvaged from a Cork City barracks during a turbulent period in Irish history. In the background is the burned-out officers' mess of Collins Barracks (formerly Victoria Barracks) on Youghal Old Road in Rathmore, County Cork.

CORK CITY
Cork
1947

An aerial photo of Cork City, featuring the National Monument on Grand Parade and the old Cork Opera House. Unfortunately, the Opera House was destroyed by fire on 13 December 1955.

Originally built in the 1850s to designs by architect John Benson, this building was called The Athenaeum when it opened in 1855. It was renamed The Munster Hall in 1875 and underwent extensive reconstruction. After that, it was renamed the Opera House in 1877.

On the left is St. Fin Barre's Cathedral, which was built in 1865. In the top right is the former Butter Market building, which was built in 1842 (now The Firkin Crane Centre), and the Shandon Bells & Tower of St. Anne's Church, one of the oldest churches in the city, dating from 1722. In the background, one can see the red brick chimney stack of the North Mall Distillery, which was founded in 1779 and destroyed by fire in 1920.

COBH

Cork

11 July 1938

The Nazi flag flying high on West Beach in Cobh during the Treaty Port handover of Spike Island on 11 July 1938, following the establishment of the Irish Free State. 'The German connection is Norddeutscher Lloyd Bremen (North German Lloyd) who operated a route from Bremen to New York via Queenstown, Cobh in the 1930s. One of the agents was the Limerick Steamship Company, hence one of the flags on the right reads LSSCo.

BEARA PENINSULA

Cork

1957

Copper miners at Allihies Mine in the Beara Peninsula in West Cork. The mines date back to 1812 when a rich copper deposit was discovered in the area. The Puxley family established the biggest copper mining enterprise in Ireland, which at its peak in 1845 employed around 1,600 people. The mines finally closed in 1962. Many Cornish miners went to Allihies to increase production, resulting in the construction of a Cornish village school and Methodist church specifically for them. The Allihies Copper Mine Museum is now housed in the former Methodist church that was built for the Cornish miners.

KILLARNEY

Kerry

c.1880

A young Kerry woman at the Gap of Dunloe in Killarney. The girl is one of the Gap Girls, who sold Poitín (Poteen) and goat's milk to tourists. Poitín, also known as Irish moonshine, is distilled from cereals, grain, whey, sugar beet, molasses and potatoes in a small pot still. The term itself is a diminutive of the Irish word 'pota', meaning 'pot'. Interestingly, the Irish word for a hangover is 'póit'.

BALLYBUNION BAY
Kerry
1880s

This photograph from the Eblana Photograph Collection features traditional Irish thatched-roof cottages and cave cliffs on White Strand, Ballybunion Bay. The curved stone-walled vegetable garden nestled amongst these cottages is particularly noteworthy.

PORTMAGEE

Kerry

c.1880

Portmagee fish curing with Valentia Island in the background. Portmagee (An Caladh, meaning 'the ferry') is a village located on the Iveragh peninsula. In the foreground, the women (all barefoot except for one) are gutting mackerel. In the background, the fish are being cured with salt and then packed in barrels to be exported by ship.

AN DAINGEAN (DINGLE) HARBOUR
Kerry
c.1890

This photo of the stunning An Daingean (Dingle) Harbour features St. Mary's Church, built in 1862, and Hussey's Folly tower in the background. In the bottom right is the Union Workhouse, which opened in 1852 on an eleven-acre site and housed up to 700 inmates. The Coastguard Station, built in 1891 and now the site of the Dingle Skellig Hotel, is visible in the background.

Hussey's Folly tower was built as a 'famine relief' project during An Gorta Mór, the Great Famine (1845–1849), as a means of providing employment for the poor. It is named after the local land agent, R. M. Hussey, who worked for the landowners, the Hickson family. Of interest in the foreground, two men are gathering hay and their family is coming to lend a hand.

KILLARNEY

Kerry

c.1890s

This photo depicts the traditional Irish thatched roof and the Cooperage in Killarney. The possible location is Bohereencael Glebe. Traditionally, a cooper is someone who makes wooden vessels held together with wooden or metal hoops.

LISSELTON

Kerry

c.1890

This photograph shows Lisselton Station on the left and Lisselton Post Office on the right. Charles Lartigue, a Frenchman, designed a steam-powered monorail that operated from 1888 to 1924, running for 9 miles between Listowel and Ballybunion. Listowel now offers a demonstration journey on a full-scale diesel-powered replica of the original monorail, and also has a Lartigue Museum.

Sceilg Mhichíl
SKELLIG MICHAEL
Kerry
c.1900

A priest outside one of the sixth-century monastic beehive-shaped huts on Skellig Michael (Sceilg Mhichíl) island, located 12km west of the Iveragh Peninsula. The stones of the building are positioned to slope outwards, allowing for wind-borne rain to run off and keep the interior watertight. The cell wall is 1.8m thick at the base, and the entrance door has a double lintel, both inside and out.

AN DAINGEAN

Kerry

c.1900

This photo shows Main Street (now Goat Street) in An Daingean (Dingle) on the Dingle Peninsula. The photo features M. McCarthy Bar (now Foxy John's pub/ hardware store) and two doors down John Atkins & Co. (now a Centra Store).

THE BALLINSKELLIGS TRANSATLANTIC CABLE STATION

Kerry

c.1900

The station was opened in 1874 by the Direct United States Cable Company, which laid a cable between Tor Bay, Nova Scotia in Canada, and Ballinskelligs. Later, the station was operated by the Anglo-American Telegraph Company, followed by Western Union. It eventually closed in 1923 as a cable station. In the 1930s and 1940s, it was used as a summer Irish language college.

The pair of barber's pole beacons were used to warn ships of the direction or line of the transatlantic cable, particularly to prevent them from dropping or dragging anchors nearby.

NENAGH CASTLE

Tipperary

c.1900

The Norman keep of Nenagh Castle was built in the 1200s by Theobald Walter. Next to it is St. Mary's Church, which was built in 1862. The church features a stained glass window by Harry Clarke, which was installed by Harry Clarke Studios in 1946 after being donated by Mrs. J. F. Read.

In 1336, James Butler, 1st Earl of Ormond, and a representative of the Irish O'Kennedy clan, signed a peace treaty at Nenagh Castle. Some 600 years later, during a 1963 state visit to Ireland, the original treaty was presented as a gift to John F. Kennedy.

CASTLE STREET, CAHIR
Tipperary
c.1900

In the background is the thirteenth-century Cahir Castle, which served as the stronghold of the powerful Butler family. On the left is Cahir House (now Cahir House Hotel), designed by William Tinsley in c.1770. It became the residence of the Earls of Glengall when the family ceased to live in Cahir Castle.

DROMINEER CASTLE

Tipperary

c.1900

Dromineer Castle, located in Dromineer on Lough Derg. Originally constructed as a hall castle in the thirteenth century near an earlier Viking fort, it was converted into a tower-house in the fifteenth century by the O'Kennedy family. The castle was later seized by Cromwellian forces in 1650.

CASHEL RAILWAY STATION
Tipperary
January 1905

Cashel Railway Station with the Rock of Cashel dramatically rising from a limestone outcrop in the Golden Vale. Brian Boru was crowned High King here in 978 and made Cashel his capital. The railway line opened in 1904, just a year before this photograph was taken. Passenger and freight services ran until its closure in 1954. Locomotive no.74, a member of the '47' Class designed at the Inchicore railway works in Dublin in 1887, served the Cashel branch line for most of its history. In the background is the fully intact Scully Cross, erected in 1870 as a memorial to the Scully family. Unfortunately, the ringed top of the cross was sheared off in 1976 when lightning struck a metal rod that ran the length of the cross. The remains now lie at the base of the cross.

THURLES SPORTSFIELD

Tipperary

8 July 1962

A moment from the 1962 Munster Hurling semi-final between Waterford and Cork. Waterford's goalkeeper, Edmond 'Ned' Power, makes a save despite the close attention of Cork's Christy Ring. The match was held in Stemple Stadium, Thurles, and resulted in a 1–16 to 4–10 victory for Waterford. The photo also features Tom Cunningham and Austin Flynn of Waterford and Liam Dowling of Cork.

Christy Ring's remarkable career with Cork spanned twenty-four years, from 1939 to 1963. He established numerous championship records, including the most career appearances (65), highest scoring tally (33–208), and eight All-Ireland medals. He is widely regarded as one of the greatest hurlers in the history of the game.

PEARSE STREET, NENAGH

Tipperary

c.1910

A busy Pearse Street (formerly Castle Street) in Nenagh. In the foreground, Nenagh's laughing lady is visible. On the left, E. T. Bourke & Co is at number 81, and another Bourke is at number 80 next to Lipton's Tea store. A sign on the store reads 'Largest Sale in the World'. Of interest in the photo is a Ford Model T with the car registration of IR-177 directly behind the cyclist wearing a straw boater hat.

KILKEE

Clare

c.1880

Featuring thatched-roof cottages in the background, along with one of M. Cahill's bathing machines (bathing boxes) in Kilkee.

Bathing machines were devices used for bathing etiquette from the eighteenth century until the early twentieth century. Bathers would change into bathing costumes in the box, which would then be pulled by a donkey to the water's edge.

MOYASTA

Clare

c.1886–1890

Sometime between 1886 and 1890 Michael Connell is evicted from his house in Moyasta. To prevent armed Royal Irish Constabulary police and British soldiers from entering, thorny bushes have been placed in the windows and doors. The Royal Irish Constabulary (RIC) was the police force in Ireland from 1822 until 1922, when the entire country was part of the United Kingdom.

The rope thatching in the photo is of interest. The thatch is not secured directly to the roof, but is held in place by a series of ropes that lie over the thatched surface and are tied to the tops of the walls or held down by large stones. This thatching method was popular along the western coast due to strong winds.

KILKEE
Clare

c.1890

This Robert French photo shows the Stella Maris Hotel in Kilkee. In the foreground, Mary Hickey's Boot, Shoemakers and Drapers Store can be seen on Queen Street (now O'Connell Street). In the background, the thatched roof of Kent's shop is visible. The Stella Maris Hotel was built in 1880, prior to the arrival of the West Clare Railway in 1892. This railway ran from Ennis to Kilkee and Kilrush on the Shannon Estuary.

BODYKE

Clare

1887

Eighty-year-old widow Margaret McNamara (in the window) along with her sons and daughters as they await the eviction party in Bodyke in 1887. The priest on the right is Fr. Peter Murphy. The eviction party consisted of members of the Royal Irish Constabulary, the 2nd Royal Welsh Fusiliers, bailiffs, and emergency men. They attacked the walls of the house with crowbars in front of a crowd of 5,000, evicting two households: those of the widow McNamara and John Liddy, who put up a noble defence.

KILRUSH
Clare
1903

Market Square and Frances Street in Kilrush. The Market House, on the right, was built by John Ormsby Vandeleur in 1808. It was burned down by the British Auxiliary Forces in 1921 and rebuilt in 1931. In the background is the Maid of Erin monument, which is dedicated to the Manchester Martyrs: Philip Allen, Michael Larkin, and Michael O'Brien, who were executed in 1867.

KILRUSH
Clare
1901

The pig fair on Merchants Quay in Kilrush, County Clare. It shows the Kilrush Wool Factory and the train terminus, which was built in 1892 and was part of the West Clare Railway. This railway ran from Ennis to Kilkee and Kilrush.

LAHINCH

Clare

c.1900

County Clare's Lahinch promenade, the beach changing huts and, in the background, the Golf Links Hotel, which opened on 5 May 1896. The hotel provides a panoramic view of the village and the Atlantic Ocean. In the background, you can also see the old church on Chapel Lane, built by Fr. Keane between 1830–1840. The present church, the Church of Our Lady of the Immaculate Conception, was constructed on a portion of the original church in November 1952 and was opened in March 1954.

ATHLUNKARD BRIDGE

Limerick

c.1880

A Jaunting Car no.107 outside the toll house at Athlunkard Bridge in Limerick City. Those entering the city from County Clare paid a halfpenny, while those with a horse and cart paid one penny; the tolls were lifted in the year 1884. The five-arch Athlunkard Bridge, spanning the Shannon, was built between June 1826 and December 1830, at a cost of £7,000, with James and Richard Paine serving as the architects. Note the two children standing at the doorway of the toll house.

PERY SQUARE
Limerick
c.1900

Pery Square in Limerick City, featuring St. Michael's Church from 1840 and the entrance to the People's Park before the Carnegie Library and Museum were built in 1908.

In the background, a freestanding column is topped by a sculpture of the influential MP Thomas Spring Rice from 1829. The statue was erected by the Barrington family, who invested heavily in this part of the city and anticipated further expansion that never came to fruition.

Also in the background is the late Georgian Gothic Revival style St. Michael's Church, designed by Limerick architect James Pain. The church was originally built without its spire and once had a capacity for 2,000 people. Interestingly, the church was known as the 'sinking church' because it was not built on bedrock and has sunk slightly over the years.

LIMERICK CITY
Limerick
1890s

Patrick Street and Rutland Street in Limerick City. The image features street vendors and elegant gas and electric street lamps. Of particular interest, Catherine Hayes, the world-famous Irish soprano of the Victorian era, also known as 'The Swan of Erin', was born at number 4 Patrick Street. On the right side of Patrick Street, at number 9–11, is the Ormston House, built in the Venetian palazzi Italianate style in 1872.

LIMERICK CITY

Limerick

c.1900

The Tait Memorial Clock in Limerick City was erected in 1867. The architect, William Edward Corbett, chose red and green coloured marble columns to commemorate Sir Peter Tait, who served as mayor of Limerick from 1866 to 1868. Tait also pioneered the production line system at his clothing factory on Edward Street in Limerick City, where he produced 50,000 American Civil War Confederate uniforms.

In the background on the right, next to the 1865 Protestant Orphan Society Hall, stands a stone and red brick building known as The Philosophical Buildings, which opened in 1843. Later renamed the Francis Ridley Havergal Memorial Hall, the hall was replaced in the 1920s by The Lyric Cinema. The cinema closed on 28 August 1976, after showing the Second World War film *Operation Daybreak*. The building was demolished in 1981.

GEORGE'S STREET

(now O'Connell Street)

Limerick

c.1900

On the left is Delaney's on the corner, with the City of Cork Steam Packet Company Limited on the first floor. In the background is the majestic Landmark Clock Tower of Cannock's Department Store (now Penney's), which was built in 1858 by architect William Fogerty. It is amazing to think that there had been a drapery shop on this site since 1814. Unfortunately, this beautiful building was demolished when Penney's took over in 1980.

BLOSSOM GATE, KILMALLOCK
Limerick
1909

This Robert French photo shows Blossom Gate on Emmet Street in Kilmallock. It is the only surviving gate of Kilmallock's 1230s medieval town defence wall. Of interest, some of the wall posters advertise Cooper's Dip (developed by veterinary surgeon William Cooper in 1852), Boys' Summer Suits by McBirney & Co., and the Gaelic Athletic Association's Annual Athletic & Cyclic Championship at Mallow on Sunday, 18 August.

MERCHANT'S QUAY
Limerick
1903

This photo from the tower of St. Mary's Cathedral in Limerick features several notable landmarks. In the foreground, the Curragower Boat Club can be seen next to the Potato Market on Merchant's Quay before the present-day clubhouse was built, although the club was founded in 1877. The Limerick Courthouse, designed by Nicholas and William Hannan in 1814, is also prominently displayed. In the background, Sarsfield Bridge (Wellesley Bridge) can be seen. This bridge was designed by Scottish engineer Alexander Nimmo in 1835. Additionally, the photo shows the 150 feet red brick chimneystack of the Condensed Milk Company of Ireland factory, built c.1860 and owned by the Cleeve brothers, which produced 60,000 cans of condensed milk each day. The factory later produced the popular confectionery Cleeve's Toffees, which continued to be sold in Ireland until the 1980s.

It is interesting to note that the photo shows the Shannon Rowing Club under construction before the building was opened in 1904.

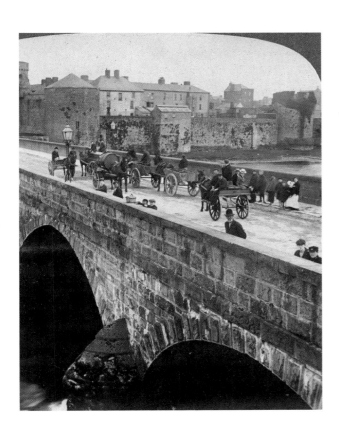

THOMOND BRIDGE
Limerick

c.1903

This photo from Underwood & Underwood shows the Thomond Bridge in Limerick City, designed by Pain Architects and completed in 1840. In the background is King John's Castle, built in 1210, with its British military barracks erected within the walls in 1751. Until 1922, it housed one hundred members of the British army and their families. Of interest, the red brick building on the upper right is Curragower House, which was also demolished like its namesake across the river on Clancy's Strand.

BRUFF
Limerick
July 1922

Children chatting with pro-Treaty national army troops on Main Street in Bruff, during the Siege of Bruff in July 1922, during the Irish Civil War. The siege involved pro- and anti-Treaty forces and lasted around 48 hours. It served as a launch pad for pro-Treaty attacks on Bruree and the famous Battle of Kilmallock, which was one of the largest engagements of the war and took place between 25 July and 5 August 1922. In the background, an item of interest is St. Peter and St. Paul's Church, which was built in 1828.

WATERFORD COURTHOUSE
Waterford
1897

A group of the Royal Irish Constabulary Committee with their bicycles outside the County Waterford Courthouse. The Royal Irish Constabulary was established in 1814, and by 1901, they had 1,600 barracks and 11,000 constables in Ireland.

LISMORE
Waterford

c.1900

This photo features the Devonshire Arms Hotel (now Lismore House Hotel) in Lismore. The monumental Gothic Revival-style fountain in the photo is the Ambrose Power Memorial, erected in 1872. It's interesting to note that the Devonshire Arms Hotel is Ireland's oldest purpose-built hotel, built by the Duke of Devonshire in 1797. Originally known as the Devonshire Arms Hotel, it provided accommodation for guests of the Cavendish family at Lismore Castle.

WATERFORD HARBOUR
Waterford
1890s

This view of Waterford Harbour showcases Waterford's maritime past on the River Suir, which for centuries served as a major artery for trade and visitors to Ireland's oldest city. In the foreground is Christ Church Cathedral, designed by local architect John Roberts in 1779. In the background is the old Timbertoes oak timber bridge, which spanned the River Suir between 1794–1910. Its narrow drawbridge was added in 1800. The Timbertoes Bridge cost £14,000 to build, which came mostly from private funding. It operated under a controversial toll until 1907 when Waterford Corporation bought it for £63,000 and abolished the toll.

STRAND STREET, TRAMORE
Waterford
1910

Strand Street in the seaside town of Tramore, featuring the Tipperary Bar & Restaurant and the novelty photography shop of 'Stickyback Powers'. Run by two sisters, the shop also sold buckets and spades. In the background, the signage of Champion Turkish Baths with Philip Morrissey as proprietor can be seen.

WATERFORD COURTHOUSE
Waterford
September 1901

In September 1901, A. H. Poole took a photo of a Jewish wedding at the County Waterford Courthouse. The bride, Ester Levin, was 22 years old and lived on John Street in Waterford. The groom, Myer Stein, was 25 years old and lived on Raymond Street in Dublin. The Waterford synagogue was located on Manor Street, not too far from the courthouse, and the steps of the courthouse were used to accommodate large group photographs.

WATERFORD CITY

Waterford

8 October 1903

Crowds on the Quays in Waterford City, showing a precarious tower of Bovril tins, and on the left is the Adelphi Hotel (now Tower Hotel), which was demolished on 25 May 1970. In the background is the Timbertoes timber bridge that spanned the River Suir between 1794–1910.

THE QUAYS, WATERFORD CITY
Waterford
16 December 1907

Carts full of Christmas turkeys queuing on the quays in Waterford City, at the foot of Conduit Lane where Messrs Flynn and Young Poultry was based. In 1908, Flynn and Young exported 10,000 turkeys to English and Scottish markets alone.

TRAMORE
Waterford
1910

The Metal Man Tower at Westtown in Tramore. The tower features children dancing around its base. The three maritime beacons at Westtown, as well as their sisters at Brownstown Head, were erected in 1823 at the behest of Lloyds of London insurance brokers. The Metal Man figure, created by Cork-born sculptor Thomas Kirk, wears the uniform of British sailors at the time of the sinking of HMS *Sea Horse* in 1816. The shipwreck resulted in the loss of 292 men, 71 women and children, with only 30 onboard surviving. Also of interest is the Metal Man located between Rosses Point and Oyster Island, which has pointed to safe passage into Sligo Harbour ever since it was first unveiled in 1821.

TRAMORE
Waterford
c.1910

The Bathing Slip in the seaside town of Tramore. In the background is Christ Church, designed by architect J. J. McCarthy in 1862. Lafcadio Hearn attended Mass at this church on Sundays. Hearn was a Greek writer, translator, and teacher who introduced the culture and literature of Japan to the West. The Japanese Gardens in Tramore are named after him.

MEAGHER'S QUAY
Waterford
22 July 1922

Irish National Army forces posing with a seized anti-Treaty mine outside the Granville Hotel on Meagher's Quay in Waterford City, during the Irish Civil War. The mines were intended to destroy the piers on the River Suir quays in the event that the Irish National Army pro-Treaty forces arrived by boat.

It is interesting to note that Irish nationalist Thomas Francis Meagher, who was born in the Granville Hotel on 5 August 1823, flew the Irish Tricolour flag for the first time on 7 March 1848, at the Wolf Tone Club on 33 The Mall in Waterford City. The flag flew continuously for eight days and nights before being removed by the authorities.

GREAT GEORGES STREET

Waterford

1926

An array of carcasses outside M. O'Regan's victuallers on number 6 Great Georges Street in Waterford City. Butcher Michael O'Regan is on the far right.

KILMEADEN CREAMERY

Waterford

31 May 1928

Gretta Sullivan, from Adamstown townland in Waterford, delivering two churns of milk to the Kilmeaden Creamery. Gretta never married, instead working as a housekeeper for her bachelor-farmer uncle, John 'The Miller' Power. Later in life, Gretta lived in Johnstown, Kilmeaden, and eventually on Summerville Avenue in Waterford, where she passed away at the age of 83 in 1985.

HENRY DOWNES & CO.

Waterford

1936

Jimmy Maher (left) and Jimmy Hennessy in the Cooperage Department of Henry Downes & Co., established in 1797 at number 10 Thomas Street, Waterford City.

In the photo Jimmy is using an air foot pump to deliver a consistent air supply to the base of the fire to aid the combustion process in the furnace. Supplying the fire with oxygen allows it to reach a temperature hot enough to manipulate and craft iron objects. On the left, the barrel that has been chalked to be 'examined' contains Jameson Whiskey (1927).

ATLANTIC
OCEAN

IRISH SEA

ULSTER

Donegal

Derry/
Londonderry

Tyrone

Antrim

Down

Fermanagh

Leitrim

Armagh

Monaghan

Mayo

Sligo

Cavan

Louth

Roscommon

Longford

Meath

CONNACHT

Westmeath

LEINSTER

Offaly

Kildare

Dublin

Galway

Wicklow

Laois

Clare

Carlow

Tipperary

Kilkenny

Wexford

Limerick

Kerry

Waterford

MUNSTER

Cork

CONNACHT

or Cúige Chonnacht *in Irish*

———————————

Galway • Mayo • Roscommon
Sligo • Leitrim

(1)

(2)

THE MODIFICATION *of* HISTORICAL PHOTOS

(3)

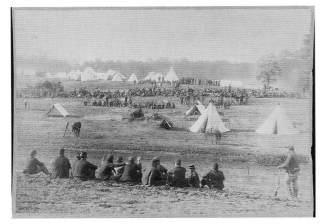

(4)

Throughout history, historical photos have been doctored by removing or adding people, even before the advent of image-editing software such as Photoshop. One example is a Library of Congress photo of US General Ulysses S. Grant on a horse at City Point in front of his troops during the American Civil War in the 1860s. According to the Library of Congress, this photograph was probably created by L. C. Handy in 1902 and is a montage of three images. It does not actually show General Ulysses S. Grant at City Point, but instead features the head of Grant at his Cold Harbor, Va. headquarters, the horse and man's body of Maj. Gen. Alexander McDowell McCook, and the background of Confederate prisoners captured in the Battle of Fisher's Hill, Va.

Another example is Adolf Hitler, who frequently had people removed from his official portraits. In one instance, he removed the chief propagandist for the Nazi Party, Joseph Goebbels, from a print that included Hitler and other friends.

PHOTOS (1) General Grant at City Point, Virginia, United States c.1902.

(2) The head, from Grant at his Cold Harbor, Va. headquarters. June 1864

(3) The horse and man's body, from Maj. Gen. Alexander McDowell McCook. July 1864

(4) The background, from Confederate prisoners captured in the battle of Fisher's Hill, Va. May 1862

(6)

This is a photo of The Four Courts (5) in Dublin City, taken on Winetavern Street during the 1922 Irish Civil War. The building had been taken over by anti-Treaty forces on 14 April and was bombarded by National Army forces artillery on 28 and 29 June, thus beginning the Irish Civil War. It should be noted that the soldier on the right with the revolver has been added to the photo. The soldier in question was cut from another 1922 Irish Civil War photo (6).

Numerous famous photographs throughout history have been heavily altered to fulfil the desires of a dictator or for other political or social reasons.

The 1917 photo (7) on the next page depicts the old Liberty Hall, which served as the Headquarters of James Larkin's Irish Transport Workers' Union in Dublin City. The photo features a banner reading 'James Connolly Murdered May 12th 1916' that was erected by four Citizen Army Women – Brigid Davis, Rosie Hackett, Helena Molony, and Jinny Shanahan – to mark the first anniversary of Connolly's death. Rosie Hackett later boasted that it took four hundred policemen to take down four women. 'We enjoyed it at the time – all the trouble they were put to.'

On the right side of the photo, a plasterer is shown repairing Liberty Hall after it was shelled by British field artillery and the admiralty gunboat, the *Helga*, during the Easter Rising. It should be noted that tricolour flags have been added to the photo at a later time.

PHOTOS (5) Winetavern Street, Dublin City during the 1922 Irish Civil War (Soldier with a revolver on the right).

(6) National Army troops at the Four Courts in Dublin City 1922 (Soldier with a revolver on the left).

(7) Old Liberty Hall, Beresford Place, Dublin City. 1917.

(7)

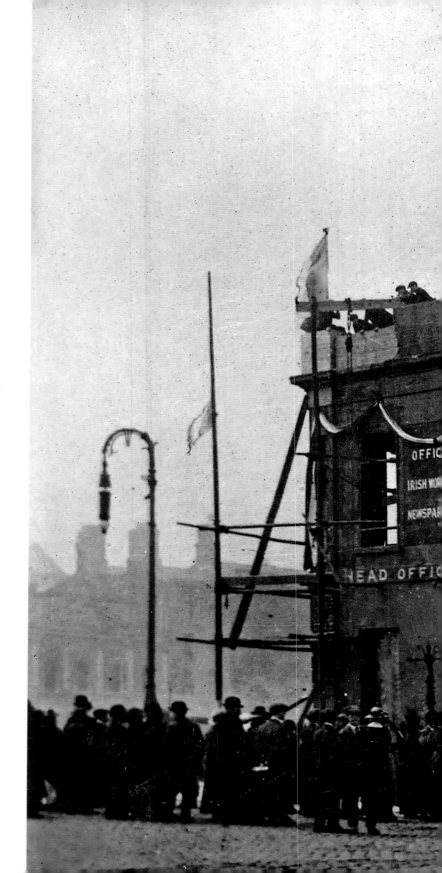

CONNEMARA
Galway
1880s

A labourer's turf hut located on the road between Letterfrack and Kylemore Abbey in Connemara. These small turf huts, which were approximately twelve feet in length, were called 'botháns'. They were built by migrant workers who worked on the land during harvest time.

CONNEMARA

Galway

1892

Three women carrying baskets of turf in Connemara. The women are using rectangular woven baskets, known in Irish as 'cliabh' (pronounced 'cleeve'), which were commonly used for carrying turf and seaweed, the latter of which was used as fertiliser for crops.

CONNEMARA
Galway
c.1892

Young boys outside a school in Connemara. It was common for Irish boys, particularly in rural areas, to wear dresses until they were twelve years old. Some of the boys in this photo are barefoot or wearing stockings without soles.

EYRE SQUARE
Galway
c.1897

Eyre Square in Galway City. Both the Imperial and Royal Hotels can be seen in the background. The Bank of Ireland is on the right, designed by architect James Cusack in 1831. On the left is an elegant electric street light standard. The 4 April 1890 edition of *The Electrical Engineer*, a weekly review of theoretical and applied electricity, states that the Galway Electrical Company was using hydroelectric power from the river Corrib to light the harbour with incandescent lamps and competed with the gas company for the public lighting of both the town and the harbour. In the background, there are also shop signs for James Joseph Ward's The Motorcycle House, Joyce Mackie & Co., and John Lenihan's merchant's store.

CONNEMARA
Galway
c.1892

The photograph depicts a family of farmers and their dog on a break in Connemara. It was taken by Major Ruttledge-Fair for the English philanthropist James Hack Tuke, who was campaigning for improved living conditions in County Donegal and Connemara. Tuke was motivated to take action after visiting Connacht in 1847, where he witnessed scenes of great distress during the Great Famine. This period of starvation and disease in Ireland lasted from 1845 to 1852, resulting in the deaths of roughly one million people and the emigration of more than one million others.

INISHMORE
Galway
c.1910

The Dillon family in Cill Éinne on Inishmore, one of the Aran Islands. In the distance to the northeast is Galway Bay. The stub in the foreground is the remains of an ancient cross at Teampall Bheanáin (Benan's Temple), which was part of a monastic settlement established by St. Enda in the sixth century. St. Enda of Aran (Éanna, Éinne, or Endeus) died around 530AD, and his feast day is celebrated on 21 March. Many of the great Irish saints had connections with Aran, and Enda was a warrior-king of Oriel in Ulster who was converted to Christianity by his sister, St. Fanchea, an abbess. Enda is known as the 'patriarch of Irish monasticism'.

CLIFDEN
Galway
c.1900

Locals gathered around the weighing station house on Market Street in the centre of the coastal town of Clifden on market day. The weighing scale tripod next to the weighing station house was used to weigh farm produce. In the background is Christ Church (Church of Ireland), which was built in 1853 to replace an earlier structure dating back to 1810. There is a freestanding limestone tomb erected in 1839 as the burial place of John D'Arcy, the founder of Clifden. He was the proprietor of a 17,000-acre estate that had been in the D'Arcy family for over 150 years. The D'Arcy family were one of the fourteen powerful families known as the Tribes of Galway.

INIS MÓR
Galway
1893

Inis Mór, one of the Aran Islands in Galway Bay, shows a prominent Celtic Cross located in Cill Rónáin, near the harbour. The cross was carved by James Pearse, the father of Pádraig Pearse and Willie Pearse, who were both executed for their part in the 1916 Rising. The thatched cottage in the background was once the home of the curate of Cill Rónáin, but it has since been replaced by a guesthouse called St. Columba's, which is now known as The Bar.

Sráid na Siopaí
SHOP STREET
Galway
c.1910

Shop Street (Sráid na Siopaí) is the main thoroughfare of the city of Galway. The photo features Buttermilk Lane and a crowded horse-drawn tram operated by the Galway and Salthill Tramway Company. The company provided a 3-foot narrow gauge passenger tramway service in Galway between 1879 and 1918. The initial six tramcars were double-deck cars manufactured by the Starbuck Car and Wagon Company. Each car required two horses to pull it. The tramway operated along a 2.13-mile (3.43km) route from the depot on Forster Street, near Galway railway station, to a terminus on the seafront at Salthill. The tramway relied heavily on the tourist trade, which was drawn by the possibility of excursions to the Aran Islands provided by the Galway Bay Steamboat Company.

FISH MARKET
Galway
1902

A Library of Congress photo shows a jolly group in the marketplace of Galway City, with the Spanish Arch visible in the background. The arch was built in 1584 as an extension of the twelfth-century Norman-built town wall. It was first known as Ceann an Bhalla ('the head of the wall'), but later became known as the Spanish Arch. In 1755, the arch was partially destroyed by a tsunami. The photo also features local businesses such as Colman Greene, John Connolly, and R. Lynskey Rope and Twine Manufacturer. Tim Shea ran a shop offering lodgings and serving as a publican. The Royal Irish Constabulary (RIC), also called the Irish Constabulary from 1836 to 1867, was the police force in Ireland from 1822 until it was disbanded on 30 August 1922. This photo is a stereoscopic card, which creates the illusion of depth by means of stereopsis for binocular vision.

GALWAY BAY

Galway

July 1954

An aerial photo from 1954, taken by Alexander 'Monkey' Campbell Morgan, of Galway Bay with the River Corrib flowing down from Lough Corrib. In the foreground are the old walls of Galway City Jail, which were demolished in 1902 and are now the site of Galway Cathedral. The bridge in the foreground was once called The Jail Bridge because it used to connect the jail on one side of the River Corrib with the courthouse on the other side. After the jail was shut down in 1902, the bridge's name was changed to the Salmon Weir Bridge. Galway Cathedral was built in 1965 on the site of the old jail, which was sold to Most Rev. Dr. Browne, Bishop of Galway, for a nominal sum of £10 by Galway County Council in 1940. In the background is the Claddagh (Cladach 'the shore') fishing district in Galway City. At its peak, the Claddagh had 468 thatched cottages that housed roughly 500 families. Due to an outbreak of tuberculosis in 1927, the cottages were replaced with council housing.

SALTHILL
Galway
c.1914

A summertime picture featuring George and Mary Mahon Dillon from Castlegar in County Galway, bathing in Salthill. Their mother was Edith Augusta Dillon, daughter of Luke Gerald Dillon, 4th Baron Clonbrock, and their father was Sir William Henry Mahon, the 5th Baronet Mahon, of Castlegar. William fought in the Boer War between 1900 and 1902 and gained the rank of Major in the 4th (Militia) Battalion, West Yorkshire Regiment. He married Edith on 26 January 1905, with whom he had five children.

KILLALA

Mayo

c.1880

The impressive twelfth-century round tower in Killala. The tower is located on an early monastic site dating back to the fifth century, where St. Patrick appointed Muiredach as the first Bishop of Killala. In the background, you can see the spire of the Cathedral Church of St. Patrick, which is one of Ireland's smallest cathedrals but also one of its oldest. It was built in the 1670s during the episcopate of Thomas Otway, Bishop of Killala and Achonry, using rubble and stone from the medieval cathedral.

ACHILL ISLAND
Mayo
c.1890s

The Achill Mission, also known as 'the Colony', at Dugort on Achill Island. St. Thomas's Church, which was designed by architect Joseph Welland in 1851, is featured in the photo, with Slievemore mountain visible in the background. In 1831, the Protestant Reverend Edward Nangle founded a proselytising mission at Dugort with the goal of spreading the gospel and converting people to Protestantism during eighteen years on the island. Rev. Nangle learned Irish in order to communicate with the islanders and regularly produced a newspaper called the *Achill Missionary Herald*. This led to conflict both within the community and externally with followers of the Archbishop of Tuam, John MacHale.

The Achill Mission included schools, cottages, an orphanage, a small hospital, and a hotel (now the Slievemore Hotel). Although several hundred people converted to Protestantism out of a population of 7,000 on Achill Island at the time, the Achill Mission slowly declined and finally closed in the 1880s. Edward Nangle passed away in 1883.

'This famine is the finger of God upon an idolatrous people'

Edward Nangle (1799–9 September 1883)

CLARE ISLAND
Mayo
c.1890s

The packing of barrels with cured fish on Clare Island sometime in the 1890s. This was then an important industry on the island. In the background is Granuaile's Castle, built in the sixteenth century by the Ó Máille (O'Malley), Kings of Umaill. The castle was a stronghold of Gráinne Ní Mháille (Grace O'Malley, c.1530–c.1603), the famous 'Pirate Queen of Ireland' who controlled a large section of the west coast of Ireland.

CLAREMORRIS
Mayo
September 1950

This photo was taken from the footbridge of Claremorris Railway Station, which opened on 19 May 1862. The two new cars being transported are Ford Prefect models produced by Ford UK between 1938 and 1961 as an upmarket version of the Ford Popular and Ford Anglia small family cars. The van in the front is a Fordson E83W, also later sold under the Thames brand and built by Ford at the Dagenham factory between 1938 and 1957.

BOYLE

Roscommon

c.1900

Main Street in Boyle, features the shopfronts of P. O'Rourke and King's. The King's shop was bought by W. T. Wynne in the 1920s, and the Wynne family still operates it almost 100 years later. In the background is Boyle Military Barracks, which was once the townhouse of the Earl of Kingston and the headquarters of the 4th Battalion of the Connacht Rangers until 1917. The entrance to Boyle Military Barracks is bustling with activity, with a soldier wearing a Scottish kilt, barefoot paperboys, and two shoeshine boxes. There are also billboard posters in the area.

BOYLE RIVER BRIDGE
Roscommon
c.1905

The triple-arch stone Boyle River Bridge was constructed in c.1864 in Boyle. In the background, you can see Nally & Cunningham's Pub & Grocery on Bridge Street, and in the upper right corner is the Boyle Military Barracks.

MARKET STREET, SLIGO TOWN
Sligo
1890s

A tailoring business (Clinchy's) with a lamppost poster seeking 'JOURNEYMEN TAILORS – WANTED – SEVERAL GOOD MEN'. In the background is the old Holy Cross (the Dominican) church on High Street peeking over the rooftops. The old church was demolished, but the former apse with its mosaics was left standing. The 'new' church was opened and dedicated on 13 May 1973. On the left-hand side of the photo is R. Gallagher's with its thatched roof, which is not typically seen in an urban setting.

CORCORAN'S MALL, SLIGO TOWN
(now John F. Kennedy Parade)
Sligo
c.1885

A packed Royal Mail and Day Car outside Walsh's Office on Corcoran's Mall (now John F. Kennedy Parade) in Sligo Town. The Day Car serviced Ballina, Bundoran, Enniskillen, Ballyshannon, and Roscommon, as indicated by the signage. Notice the small stepladder on the bottom right of the photo, which was used to help people get on board the horse-drawn carriage.

LOUGH GILL

Sligo

c.1900

A herd of cattle at Lough Gill in Sligo. In the background is an Aermotor windmill that was used to pump water to Hazelwood House, an eighteenth-century Palladian-style mansion located in a 70-acre demesne in the parish of Calry.

KILFREE

Sligo

May 1960

A man pushing a steam locomotive around a railway turntable at Kilfree Junction in County Sligo. This was one of the last mainline 2-4-0 steam locomotives still running in Europe. The pit of the turntable is still in place and now forms part of the garden of the old station house at Kilfree.

Kilfree Junction railway station was opened by the Sligo and Ballaghderreen Railway on 31 October 1874. It became part of the Midland Great Western Railway (MGWR) in 1877. The station closed on 4 February 1963 along with the branch line.

GLENCAR
Leitrim
1900

Glencar with Slievemore Mountain (An Sliabh Mór), also known as King's Mountain, in the background. The left hand picture shows Glencar Lake with Slievemore Mountain further in the background.

GARADICE

Leitrim

1959

Men working on the permanent way, lifting narrow-gauge railway tracks from the Cavan and Leitrim Railway (C&LR) at Garadice. The railway, which opened in 1887, was closed by Córas Iompair Éireann (CIÉ) in 1959.

BALLINAMORE

Leitrim

28 April 1959

Ballinamore Railway Station in Leitrim features the Cavan and Leitrim Railway (C&LR) 2-6-0T locomotive no.3T. This locomotive was originally part of the Tralee and Dingle Light Railway, but was transferred to the Cavan and Leitrim line in the 1950s when the Dingle line closed.

The Ballinamore to Arigna Coal Mines route on the Cavan and Leitrim Railway was a narrow-gauge railway that operated from 1887 until 1959.

ULSTER

or Cúige Uladh *in Irish*

Donegal • Tyrone • Antrim • Down
Derry/Londonderry • Cavan • Fermanagh
Armagh • Monaghan

THE USE OF
WOMEN *in* WAR
PROPAGANDA

This photograph, taken by Irish Press photojournalist Colman Doyle in 1973, depicts a long-haired woman IRA volunteer in a polka dot dress carrying an AR18 assault rifle while on active service in West Belfast. It has become one of the most iconic images of the Troubles and has appeared in numerous newspapers, calendars, and on merchandise such as mugs and t-shirts.

It is claimed to have been taken in either Ardoyne or West Belfast. Doyle himself claims that he doesn't

remember the location and states that the photo was not staged. However, there is an image of three IRA women that appeared in the Belfast-based *Republican News* in February 1974, and again in a 1974 Republican Resistance calendar, which features the same long-haired woman in a polka dot dress carrying an assault rifle. This suggests that these photos were part of a set of propaganda photos aimed at attracting women to join the IRA.

In the past, propaganda has been used as a tool by governments and militaries to shape public opinion and support for conflicts. The use of women in propaganda campaigns, portrayed in various roles, including soldiers, nurses, and mothers, to evoke emotions and create a moral imperative for war, is a common propaganda tactic. The iconic "Rosie the Riveter" image during the Second World War portraying a strong and empowered woman working in a factory to support the war effort, is a particularly famous example.

However, the use of women in war propaganda is not without controversy, as it can reinforce harmful gender stereotypes and objectify women. It is important to consider the broader implications of these representations and promote more equitable and inclusive representations of women in wartime propaganda.

BALLYSHANNON

Donegal

1870s

This image features the 1842 St. Anne's Church and the 10-arch Allingham Bridge on the River Erne, which was demolished in the 1940s. St. Anne's Church of Ireland churchyard is situated on the high hill of Mullach na Sí (Hill of the Fairies), overlooking the panorama of 'Saimer's Green Vale'. The church was designed by William Farrel in the Saxon style of architecture and completed in 1842, replacing the old church of 1795. In the foreground of the photograph is the Ballyshannon fishing weir, with its thatched roof hut and hanging fishing nets, long before the Cathaleen's Fall Hydro Station was built in 1946.

The Allingham Memorial Bridge was demolished in the 1940s, and the course of the river was changed to allow for the production of electricity at Cathaleen's Falls. On the bridge, there is a plaque commemorating one of Ballyshannon's native poets, William Allingham (1824–1889).

COCKHILL

Donegal

c.1880

St. Mary's Church, which was built in 1847 in Ballymacarry, Cockhill near Buncrana. The Cockhill waterwheel and mill house are visible on the left, and the Cockhill school is visible on the right.

IRISH EVICTION

Donegal

1890s

The aftermath of an eviction in Donegal. The evicted tenants are outside their hut, surrounded by their belongings. It is estimated that between 250,000 and 500,000 Irish families were evicted from their homes during the Famine years. Landlords raised rents to unsustainable levels, a practice known as rent-racking. This forced tenants into arrears, and allowed landlords by law to evict them without compensation for the work they had done.

GWEEDORE

Donegal

1887

An evicted family with their baby in a crib in Gaoth Dobhair (Gweedore). Gweedore is officially known by its Irish name, Gaoth Dobhair. 'Gaoth' refers to an inlet of the sea at the mouth of the River Crolly, which is known as An Ghaoth.

GLENTIES
Donegal
c.1890s

A rope-thatched hut located next to the Dry Arch bridge in Straboy, Glenties. In the foreground, a woman can be seen knitting next to a spring water well covered in turf.

BUNCRANA
Donegal
c.1900

A water wheel in Cockhill, Buncrana. Buncrana (Bun Cranncha) means 'foot of the (River) Crana'.

LOUGH SWILLY

Donegal

c.1900

The British Royal Navy Artillery fleet anchored in Lough Swilly at Rathmullan on the Fanad Peninsula. This location was the scene of the Flight of the Earls in 1607. In the background, The Battery can be seen, which was built in 1810 as one of six on the shores of Lough Swilly. It is one of many defensive structures built by the British in the wake of the French invasion of 1798 in support of the United Irishmen's rebellion. In the far distance is the village of Fahan (Fathain Mura, meaning 'little green/field of Mura'), which is a district of Inishowen in the north of County Donegal.

CARDING WOOL

Donegal

1900

A photo by Robert French for Cottage Industries shows a woman carding wool with bare feet. Carding wool is the process of separating and preparing wool fibres (or cotton, for that matter) for spinning.

OWENCARROW VIADUCT

Donegal

1900

This photograph depicts Locomotive 4–6–2T no.14 on the Owencarrow railway viaduct of the old Derry/Londonderry and Lough Swilly Railway line in County Donegal. The Londonderry and Lough Swilly Railway (L&LSR) ran from Derry to Burtonport via Letterkenny, and the Owencarrow Viaduct was located between Barnes Gap and Creeslough.

On 30 January 1925, the Owencarrow Viaduct disaster occurred on the Londonderry and Lough Swilly Railway (L&LSR) when winds of up to 120mph derailed Locomotive 4–6–2T no.14 carriages from the viaduct, causing it to partially collapse. The roof of one carriage was ripped off, leading to the deaths of four people who were thrown from the train. The four individuals killed were Philip Boyle and his wife Sarah from Arranmore Island, Una Mulligan from Falcarragh, and Neil Duggan from Meenbunowen, Creeslough.

An Craoslach
CREESLOUGH
Donegal
c.1900

A photograph of the local community gathered outside the Post Office on Main Street in the village of Creeslough (An Craoslach). On 7 October 2022, an explosion in Creeslough destroyed a shop, an Applegreen petrol station, and the adjoining apartment block, resulting in ten deaths and multiple injuries.

MALIN HEAD
Donegal
January 1902

The opening of the Marconi Wireless Telegraph Station next to the 1884 Malin Tower (Lloyds Signal Semaphore Station) in Malin Head. The photo is of interest due to the workmen on the roof with their tools. The roof was blown off during the Stephen's Day storm in 1998. Despite being made of reinforced concrete, it was ripped straight off by wind gusts of up to 111mph.

DOWNINGS
Donegal
c.1910

Fishermen and baskets of herring on the pier at Downings (Na Dúnaibh) on the Rosguill Peninsula. In the background, barrels of salted fish can be seen, as well as women working.

PETTIGO

Donegal

1924

This is a still taken from British Pathé footage titled *The Seat of all the Trouble! First pictures from the much debated Ulster Border.* It features the Free State's National Army and a constable of the Royal Ulster Constabulary at the bridge over the Termon River in Pettigo.

COALISLAND

Tyrone

1901–1911

A photo of the square in Coalisland features businesses such as Lytle Undertaking & Posting Establishment, F. V. Fullen, J. McMahon (butcher), and G. Patterson (hardware merchant). On the right are the square's water pump and horse-drinking trough.

DUNGANNON

Tyrone

c.1900

Scotch Street in Dungannon (Dún Geanainn, 'Geanann's fort'), with the Hill of the O'Neill and Ranfurly House on Market Square visible in the background. The O'Neills were one of the most powerful dynasties in Ulster, ruling the region for over 400 years.

From 1232 until 1616, the O'Neills were the sovereign kings of Tír Eógain, holding territories in the north of Ireland, particularly around modern-day County Tyrone, County Derry, and County Antrim, in the province of Ulster.

Notably, some of the local businesses at the time included T. W. Reynolds Druggist & Grocer, T. Cullen Provision Store, Roberts Lodgings, Gray Ironmonger & Grocer.

GLENARM

Antrim

1860–1883

The Glenarm River in Glenarm, featuring the Church of St. Patrick in the parish of Tickmacrevan. The church, which is located near the town and occupies the site of an ancient monastery, was built in 1768. It was financed by the noble family of McDonnell and was later enlarged in 1822 with a loan of £500 from the late Board of First Fruits.

BALLYMENA

Antrim

c.1880s

The Harryville Motte and Bailey in Ballymena. In the twelfth century, the Anglo-Normans built wooden forts on top of these large defensive earth mounds called mottes. In the foreground, a man is using a scythe, an agricultural implement for mowing grass or harvesting crops. Next to him, one can see his whetstone, a stone used for sharpening the scythe's blade.

BALLYMENA
Antrim

c.1890s

The stacking of turf in Ballymena. During the summer months, people would harvest the turf from the bogs, cutting sod to dry away from the turf bank before stacking it into reeks. Of note, the barefooted boy sitting down has a bandaged foot.

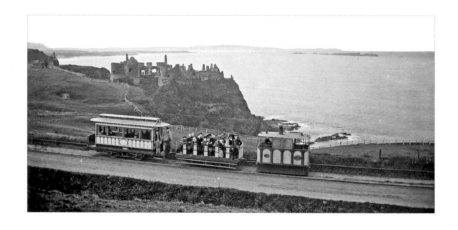

DUNLUCE CASTLE
Antrim
1890s

The Giant's Causeway Tramway, the first railway line in the world to be powered by hydroelectricity, with Dunluce Castle in the background. The line opened from Portrush to Bushmills in 1883, then extended to the Causeway in 1887 before closing in 1949. In 2002, the Giant's Causeway and Bushmills Railway was constructed over the final two miles of the original Tramway, carrying its first passengers during Easter of that year.

Dunluce Castle (Dún Libhse) was constructed in the late Middle Ages and seventeenth century, and served as the seat of Clan MacDonnell. It rests on the edge of a basalt outcropping in Antrim, between Portballintrae and Portrush, and is accessible via a bridge connecting it to the mainland.

BELFAST

Antrim

c.1900

The High Street in Belfast. The photo includes horse-drawn carriages, Sawer's food store (established as a family business in 1897), and in the background, the sandstone Albert Memorial Clock Tower completed in 1869 which stands at a height of 34.4 metres. Albion Cloth Company is located next to Sawer's, and on the right is a row of Forster Green & Co. Tea Merchants' carriages. Belfast's first trams were horse-drawn and operated by the Belfast Street Tramways Company in 1872. The service was replaced by diesel buses on 10 February 1954, when the last tram ran. It is interesting to compare the busy High Street in Belfast c.1900 with the aftermath of the German Luftwaffe bombardment on the night of 15/16 April 1941 and another bombing raid on the night of 4/5 May.

GIANT'S CAUSEWAY

Antrim

c.1900

A gentleman observing some of the 40,000 interlocking basalt columns at the Giant's Causeway. The area was declared a World Heritage Site by UNESCO (United Nations Educational, Scientific and Cultural Organization) in 1986.

CAUSEWAY

Antrim

1900

The Causeway Hotel, built by Elizabeth Henry in 1836, is on the left, and Kane's Royal Hotel is on the right. Both hotels provided accommodation for travellers visiting the Giant's Causeway. In the centre of the photo is the Causeway School, now known as The Nook. Soldier Robert Quigg (1885–1955) attended this school from 1893–1898. He was awarded the Victoria Cross for his 'most conspicuous bravery' in rescuing seven soldiers from no man's land at the Battle of the Somme on 1 July 1916.

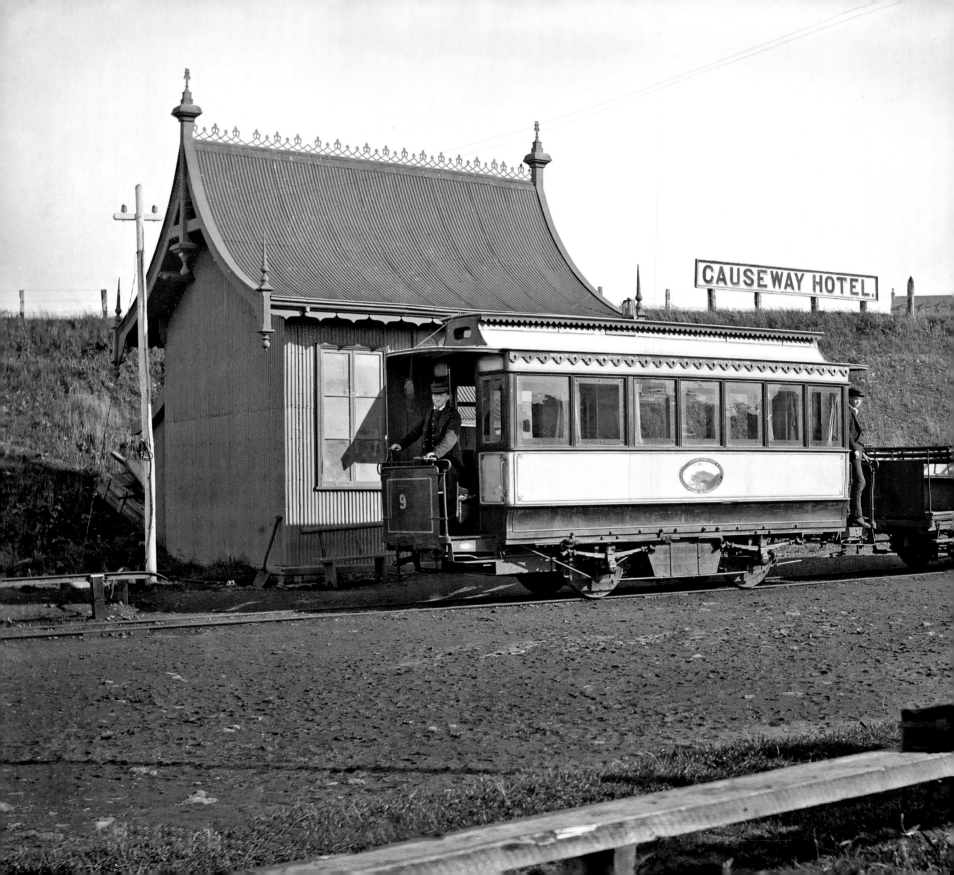

CAUSEWAY

Antrim

c.1900

The narrow gauge Giant's Causeway Tram. The tram was powered by hydroelectricity and opened from Portrush to Bushmills in 1883, extending to Causeway in 1887. It ceased operations in 1949.

The Giant's Causeway Tramway was a pioneering narrow gauge electric railway operated by the Giant's Causeway, Portrush and Bush Valley Railway & Tramway Company Ltd. Steam tram engines were used for the Portrush to Bushmills passenger traffic, as electric power could not be provided in the town section of Portrush. This was because the original electric power was fed to the trains via an elevated third rail that ran alongside the line. In the background of the photo, Kane's Royal Hotel can be seen, which was built in the c.1890s and has since been demolished.

Of note, the leather camera case seen on the bench was used to carry the glass plate camera used by Robert French, who was the chief photographer of the William Lawrence Photographic Studios based on Sackville Street (now O'Connell Street) in Dublin.

PORTRUSH PENINSULA

Antrim

c.1890s

A small, sheltered beach on the east side of the Portrush Peninsula, located between the Blue Pool and the Salmon Fishery. Known as 'Murtagh's Mouth', this beach was one of two Ladies' Bathing Places in the area, the other being at Craigvara or Arcadia Strand. The gentlemen swam in the Blue Pool, which also had diving facilities. In 1934, the harbour hosted an international water polo match between Wales and Ireland, as well as the race for the mile swimming championship of Ireland.

BALLYMENA

Antrim

1910

Church Street in Ballymena, featuring businesses such as Matthew Montgomery's Carriage and Motor Works, Johnston's Sight Testing Rooms, and John McDowell's Boots and Shoes.

BELFAST

Antrim

February 1912

The *Olympic*, after losing a port propeller blade in February 1912. Shipbuilder Thomas Andrews, head of the drafting department for Harland and Wolff, the company that built the ship, and also the chief designer of RMS *Titanic*, is featured in the foreground on the left.

On 24 February, at around 4:26PM, the ship struck a submerged, derelict, wooden-hulled vessel about 750 miles off the coast of Newfoundland. After passengers and cargo had disembarked, the ship arrived in Southampton a day later than scheduled. The *Olympic* continued her journey at a reduced speed and then returned to Harland & Wolff's in Belfast for repairs. This work delayed the completion of the *Titanic* and postponed her maiden voyage by about three weeks.

It's worth noting that on 14 April 1912, the then-*Olympic* offered to take on the survivors of the *Titanic*. However, Captain Rostron of Cunard's RMS *Carpathia* turned down the offer because he was concerned that asking the survivors to board a virtual mirror image of *Titanic* would cause them distress.

BALLYCASTLE

Antrim

1920

The collapsed column across the Grey Man's Path (Fhir Leith) Gully at Fair Head, Ballycastle. The area is steeped in myth and legend, including The Grey Man's Path. According to the myth, the Grey Man is a spectre that appears when the mist rolls in from the sea and takes human form, wandering up this gully.

ROSTREVOR VILLAGE

Down

c.1900

People on a bridge over the Kilbroney River in Rostrevor Village. The name 'Rostrevor' comes from the Irish 'Ros', meaning 'wooded headland', and 'Trevor', from the seventeenth-century Trevor family.

STRANGFORD

Down

c.1890s

Strangford village at the mouth of Strangford Lough. Strangford Castle was built in the sixteenth century to guard the entrance to the lough. In the background, one can see the red door of H. F. Quayle's Weighbridge and Weighbridge Office.

PORTSTEWART HARBOUR

Derry/Londonderry

c.1900

The Promenade at Portstewart Harbour. Portstewart was founded in 1792 by John Cromie, who named it after his maternal ancestors, the Stewarts of Ballylesse. In the background, locals can be seen chatting outside S. R. Henry Groceries on The Promenade, next to the Carrig-na-Cule Family Hotel.

THE BOGSIDE
Derry/Londonderry
1971

Colman Doyle took this photo of a 1971 protest in Derry against internment without trial. The photo shows some children and individuals carrying petrol bombs. Notably, these are the same streets in the Bogside where Martin McGuinness, an Irish Republican politician and statesman for Sinn Féin and a leader within the Provisional Irish Republican Army, was born.

TINTOWN ESTATE
Derry/Londonderry
1950s

This Colman Doyle photo from the 1950s features children from the Tintown Estate, which was formerly a US Army camp. It became home for Catholic families who were moved there as a 'temporary' solution to the post-Second World War housing shortage.

DERRY
Derry/Londonderry
1971

John Hume being detained by a British soldier in Derry, in 1971. John won the Nobel Peace Prize in 1998 and is regarded as one of the architects of the Northern Ireland peace process. It is true what they say: behind every great man is a great woman, and Pat Hume was that woman.

DERRY
Derry/ Londonderry
30 January 1972

Eight days before the notorious 'Bloody Sunday', a photo was taken of the Magilligan Anti-Internment Rally in Derry, featuring John Hume speaking to a soldier from the British Army's Parachute Regiment. The Northern Ireland Civil Rights Association (NICRA) organised the anti-Internment protest at Magilligan internment camp on the north coast of County Derry.

John Hume (18 January 1937–3 August 2020) stated, 'I thought that I had a duty to help those that weren't as lucky as me.'

BELTURBET

Cavan

c.1900

The old Market House, with the Working Men's Hall overlooking The Diamond, and the last of nineteenth-century urban thatched roofs on Main Street in Belturbet. Farm produce of all kinds was weighed and sold on the ground floor, and the first floor was used as the administration area for the corporation. The weekly Court of Pye was also held here every Saturday. In 1927, the Market House was demolished, and the present Town Hall was built on the site.

On the right-hand side is A. Strain's shop, which has a hand sign for Rudge Whitworth Cycles.

Of interest, on 28 December 1972, the Belturbet bombing occurred when a car bomb planted by Loyalist paramilitaries exploded in the main street. The bomb killed two teenagers, Geraldine O'Reilly (aged 15) and Patrick Stanley (aged 16).

KILLCONNY QUAY

Cavan

c.1880

The 174-passenger Steam Ship *Belturbet* operated a passenger service between Belturbet and Enniskillen until its hull was melted down for the First World War effort. The SS *Belturbet* service was run in conjunction with the G.N.R.I Railway company, which provided special trains from Dublin's Amiens Street Terminus (now Connolly Station) to Belturbet Station. From there, passengers walked to the existing Killconny Quay, where they boarded the Steam Ship *Belturbet*.

BELTURBET

Cavan

c.1900

The spire of the Gothic Revival Church of Ireland built in 1828 can be seen in the background. Belturbet (Béal Tairbirt, meaning 'mouth of the isthmus') historically served as one of the best places to cross the River Erne. It was a thriving urban centre whose prosperity relied heavily on its location along the river.

BELLEEK
Fermanagh
1897

Fishermen at the old Belleek Sluice Gates, also known as Flood Gates. These gates were erected in 1883 on the River Erne in Belleek. They consisted of four draw-doors, each weighing 13 tons. The Belleek Sluice Gates were demolished in the 1950s as part of the Erne Hydroelectric scheme.

BELLEEK
Fermanagh

c.1900

A busy fair day on Main Street in Belleek. Hand slapping is in full swing, with deals being made and cattle being bought and sold. Belleek village was first laid out on the banks of the River Erne during the Plantation of Ulster in about 1610.

LURGAN
Armagh
1930

A bird's eye view of Lurgan, featuring the Gas Works gasometers, Lurgan Model Primary School, the chimney stack of the James Johnston and Joseph Allen power loom factory built in 1888 and capable of housing 500 looms, and St. Peter's Church, built in 1832.

The Lurgan Gasworks was constructed on the site of the old Bridewell or jail on William Street, which was built in 1831.

St. Peter's Church was built in 1829, possibly in response to the Catholic Emancipation Act of 1829. Charles Brownlow provided an appropriate site on North Street for the Very Reverend William O'Brien, Parish Priest, to build a parish church.

ARMAGH CITY

Armagh

1865–1914

The view of Armagh City from atop the tower of the Church of Ireland St. Patrick's Cathedral. The photo features the twin spires of the St. Patrick's Cathedral, which was built in various phases between 1840 and 1904. Also visible is Shambles Market, which was designed by hometown architect Francis Johnston in 1827.

BALLYBAY
Monaghan
c.1905

This photo from Underwood & Underwood shows girls playing 'Green grow the rushes–O' while boys do gymnastic exercises and the teacher watches during recess outside of Ballidian National School in Ballybay. The school was originally known as 'Balladinaw' and was established in 1829.

CLONES

Monaghan

1960

This photo captures the mid–demolition state of Platform no.1 at Clones Train Station in County Monaghan. The station was opened in 1858 by GNRI (Great Northern Railway Ireland) and closed to passenger traffic on 14 October 1957. It is of interest that Barry McGuigan, an Irish boxing promoter and former featherweight world champion known as the Clones Cyclone, has family connections to the Clones Railway. His grandfather James McGuigan, his father Paddy McGuigan and one of his brothers, Kevin McGuigan, worked on the railway. Following the station's closure, his father became a musician and vocalist while his brother Kevin became a master carpenter.

Notes on
PHOTOGRAPHERS

William Mervyn Lawrence and Robert French

In 1865, at the age of 24, Dubliner William Mervyn Lawrence (1840–1931) set up his photographic studio at his mother's toy shop at 7 Upper Sackville Street, right across the road from the General Post Office. After losing his right arm in an accident, Lawrence employed his brother John Fortune Lawrence as an assistant photographer, and he developed the stereo photographs side of the business.

In 1880 the dry-plate process arrived and by then William had a team of printers and colourists working for him when he employed Robert French (1841–1917), who had briefly been in the Royal Irish Constabulary stationed in Glenealy, County Wicklow. French first was employed as a printer before working his way up to a colourist and finally becoming William's chief photographer.

The 1890s saw William's business of the colouring of postcards take off. One could argue that this success helped fund French to use his camera to photograph some 30,000 glass-plate negatives the length and breadth of Ireland, before his retirement in 1914, images which help document Ireland's history. He didn't know it at the time, but French would become the foremost visual history chronicler of his generation in providing an invaluable visual record of urban and rural Ireland.

Arthur Henri Poole

Originally from Taunton, Somerset, in the south of England, Arthur Henri Poole was born in 1850. In the 1880s he moved to Waterford City, where he set up Waterford Photographic Company. Poole produced some 65,000 glass negatives documenting the social and economic life of Waterford and the south-east of Ireland from the 1880s onwards. In 1928 Poole left a note saying he was going to Tramore, a popular seaside resort seven miles from Waterford City, after which he disappeared mysteriously.

Herbert Walter Doughty

In 1908 Herbert Walter Doughty was the *Manchester Guardian*'s first staff photographer. He was sent to Cork in December 1920 to document the sheer destruction caused by British forces during the Irish War of Independence following the burning of Cork on 11 December 1920. Later on, Herbert was sent to Dublin to cover the Irish Civil War (1922–23) with a camera he had custom-built for his use.

W. D. Hogan

W. D. Hogan was a commercial and press photographer located in Henry Street in Dublin between 1920 and 1935. Hogan produced 160 photographs between June and July 1922, visually documenting a violent and turbulent period in Dublin during the early stages of the Irish Civil War.

James P. O'Dea

James P. O'Dea was a devoted railway enthusiast, and his subjects include locomotives, railway stations and bridges, as well as railway staff and passengers. His work documents all aspects of railway transportation in Ireland between 1937 and 1977, where he photographed several railway stations and lines on the extensive Irish rail network before it was unfortunately dismantled at an alarming rate. Ireland's extensive rail network, at its peak in 1920, had 3,500 route miles, but in the 1950s and 1960s large swathes of routes were closed and today the total network is a mere 1,698 route miles.

The Dillon Family

The Dillon family were the Barons Clonbrock from Ahascragh in County Galway. As a family of enthusiastic amateur photographers, their glass-plate photographs provide an invaluable visual record of urban and rural Ireland over a period spanning the years from 1860 to 1930.

Colman Doyle

Colman Doyle was a photographer from Dalkey, Dublin, who worked for *The Irish Press* from 1951 until the newspaper ceased publication in 1995. For forty years, he also worked for the French magazine *Paris Match* from Ireland. Doyle is renowned for his photojournalism, which depicts political and social scenes in Ireland and Northern Ireland from the 1950s to 2000. He documented almost every major historical event in Ireland over a fifty-year period, as well as several world leaders, including John F. Kennedy, Charles de Gaulle, Éamon de Valera, Seán Lemass, Princess Grace, Pope John Paul II, and Charlie Chaplin. In 2006, he donated his collection of over 25,000 photographs to the National Library of Ireland. Colman is now retired in Ballyknockan, County Wexford.

LOCATIONS INDEX

RESOURCES

Transformation of the Dublin Docklands:

Caul, I. (2018) Bringing it back to basics: The Dublin Docklands – Cities for whom?, *Planet Geography* (online). Available at: www.planetgeogblog.wordpress.com/2018/02/13/bringing-it-back-to-basics-the-dublin-docklands-cities-for-whom (Accessed: 26/05/2023).

Grand Canal Dock. (April 2023). *Wikipedia*. Available at: https://en.wikipedia.org/wiki/Grand_Canal_Dock (Accessed: 26/05/2023).

The Use of Women in War Propaganda:

Ó Néill, J. (2020) The camera doesn't lie?, *The Treason Felony Blog* (online). Available at: https://treasonfelony.wordpress.com/2020/05/19/the-camera-doesnt-lie/ (Accessed: 26/05/2023).

Reinisch, D. (2022) The story behind and iconic Troubles' photo, *RTÉ* (online). Available at: https://www.rte.ie/brainstorm/2020/0616/1147804-troubles-northern-ireland-colman-doyle-photo-woman-ira-belfast-1973/ (Accessed: 26/05/2023).

The Modification of Historical Photos:

7 Historical Photos You Didn't Were Modified (May 2023). *FuturaPhoto*. Available at: https://futuraphoto.com/blog/7-historical-photos-you-didn-t-know-were-modified/ (Accessed: 26/05/2023).

Dorney, J. (2015) Weapons of the Irish Revolution Part III – The Civil War 1922-23, *The Irish Story* (online). Available at: https://www.theirishstory.com/2015/05/21/weapons-of-the-irish-revolution-part-iii-the-civil-war-1922-23/#.ZD8bWXbMLQN (Accessed: 26/05/2023).

The Irish Times Archives
www.irishtimes.com

Dublin City Library
www.dublincity.ie/residential/libraries

Irish Architectural Forum
www.archiseek.com

National Library of Ireland
www.nli.ie

National Library of Ireland on The Commons
www.flickr.com/photos/nlireland

Dictionary of Irish Architects 1720–1940
www.dia.ie

Ordnance Survey of Ireland Spatial Data
www.geohive.ie

Google Earth
earth.google.com

IMAGE CREDITS

THANK YOU TO ...

Two deep-learning programmers, Jason Antic and Dana Kelley, for creating the DeOldify software and for their encouragement throughout my Bringing Ireland's History to Life project.

All the staff at Black & White Publishing, and at Gill Hess.

Joe Duffy for his introductory essay that begins this book.

The brilliant historian Donal Fallon for all the support and encouragement over the years.

The staff at the National Library of Ireland and all the contributors to their Flickr page.

All the helpful and friendly staff of libraries throughout Ireland.

Paul Clerkin and his brilliant Archiseek website.

The staff of *The Irish Times* and all the journalists who supported my project.

All my Twitter followers for their encouragement and support throughout this journey.

ABOUT ROB CROSS

Rob Cross hails from Limerick City in Ireland and has a professional background in architecture and digital technology. He graduated from Edinburgh's Heriot-Watt University and now works for an award-winning architectural practice in Dublin City.

Rob is passionate about Irish history, particularly preserving its architectural heritage and culture. In his project 'Bringing Ireland's History to Life' Rob meticulously restores and colourises historical photos for future generations to enjoy. What began as a hobby is now captured in this book. Rob's debut book was a bestseller, and he has appeared on national TV and radio, including RTÉ's Nationwide programme. His work has been featured in exhibitions at Dublin's Custom House and Mansion House, as well as at the Crawford Art Gallery in Cork. The history project also has an international fanbase on Twitter, including politicians.

@RobCross247 | #TheColourOfIreland
thecolourofireland.com | robcrossphotography.com

ALSO AVAILABLE

The Colour of Ireland:
County by County 1860–1960

large format
978-1-78530-364-7
small format
978-1-78530-460-6

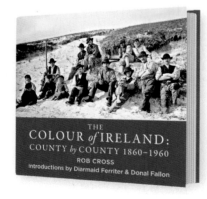

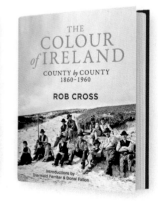